WITHDRAWN

P9-CAB-875

Fire Up Your Life in Retirement

101 Ways for Women to Reinvent Themselves

Fire Up Your Life in Retirement

101 Ways for Women to Reinvent Themselves

Catherine DePino, Ed.D.

Paragon House
St. Paul, Minnesota

Carol Stream Public Library
Carol Stream, Illinois 60188-1634

First Edition 2014

Published in the United States by
Paragon House
1925 Oakcrest Avenue
St. Paul, MN 55113

Copyright © 2014 by Catherine DePino

All rights reserved. No part of this book may be reproduced, in any form, without written permission from the publisher, unless by a reviewer who wishes to quote brief passages.

Library of Congress Cataloging-in-Publication Data

DePino, Catherine.
  Fire up your life in retirement : 101 ways for women to reinvent themselves / by Catherine DePino, Ed.D.
    p. cm.
  Summary: "Covers 101 topics helpful to women about to retire or in the midst of retirement such as financial planning, second careers, hobbies, health issues, emotional and physical challenges, nourishing friendships, and living a meaningful life"--Provided by publisher.
  ISBN 978-1-55778-911-2 (pbk.)
  1. Women--Retirement. 2. Retirement--Planning. I. Title.
  HQ1062.D46 2014
  306.3'8082--dc23
                                    2013042463

E-book ISBN: 978-1-61083-085-0

The paper used in this publication meets the minimum requirements of American National Standard for Information Sciences—Permanence of Paper for Printed Library Materials, ANSIZ39.48-1984.

Manufactured in the United States of America
10 9 8 7 6 5 4 3 2 1

For current information about all releases from Paragon House,
visit the web site at: www.ParagonHouse.com

506.38082

DEP

Dedication

To Dr. C. Monica Uhlhorn: dear Aunt, esteemed
educator, and lifelong role model, who knows
better than anyone how to live every moment
of her life to the fullest

*"Does anyone ever realize life while they live it—
every, every minute?"*—Emily, *Our Town*

5\14

Acknowledgements

I want to thank Rosemary Yokoi, my editor, for her expertise in helping prepare this book for publication. She was always available to answer questions, and I am grateful for her enthusiasm and encouragement along the way. I would also like to thank Dr. Gordon L. Anderson, president of Paragon House, for his kindness and helpful input.

Contents

Introduction

How to Use This Book

Imagine if you could live your life exactly the way you wanted to each day. You could get up when you wanted, stay up as late as you wanted, and have the freedom to work, play, or enjoy a favorite hobby whenever you felt like it. What would it be like if you didn't have to follow a strict schedule or kowtow to your boss's every command?

Whether you had a career and a family or stayed home to raise your kids, didn't have kids and spent your days moving up the career ladder, or remained single and spent your time concentrating on your job, you have something in common with the other readers of this book. You never seemed to have time for you. Now is that time. This book offers friendly advice, from one woman to another, about how to make your dreams a reality, dreams you never had time for when you were tied up in the workplace, in your home, or both.

Now you're beginning to live the best half of your life. You're about to retire or else you've retired already and you're still trying to decide what to do with the rest of your life. You have decisions to make, and that's not always easy.

You'd like to see yourself doing all the things you've dreamed about but never had time for. You probably already know this, but facing the second half of your life can prove more daunting than working outside or inside your home ever did. Uncertainty always unsettles us. But the anticipation of what's to come can also buoy us up. All you have to do is open yourself up to it and say, "I'm ready. This is my time to do what I've always wanted. And if I don't do it now, I may never do it."

What exactly will you do with all that extra time when you retire? Will things change between you and your significant other now that you're spending more time together? What will it be like in the romance department? How will you structure your days? How will you deal with medical issues, boredom, fears, and loneliness?

Will your relationship with your kids and grandkids (if you don't have kids consider your relationships with your family and friends) stay the same or evolve into something completely different and more rewarding? If you still have your parents, how will they fit into the picture? Of course, you have your own set of questions, and you'll seek solutions that will prove most helpful to you.

Some people think of the word *retirement* as an ending and live the rest of their lives sitting around and watching the world go by instead of making a plan and then living their lifelong dreams. But you're not the kind of person who believes that. If you were, you wouldn't have chosen this book. You know in your heart that the fun is just beginning. And oh, what an adventure it will be!

Does it sound hard to believe? Stay with me. This book will give you practical tips and ideas to make these years the most satisfying time of your life. Browse through it for instant inspiration when you need a gentle shove to help you implement your plan to live the best life ever, the life you've waited for.

Choose any way you want to digest the information in this book. You're totally in charge. Interact with it, write on its pages, and talk to yourself or a friend about it. Agree, disagree, and come up with your own exciting ideas. Each day, choose a section or a single topic in the book to jumpstart your plan to enjoy every moment of every day. The topics will help you seek solutions to many of the issues you'll face in your life as a future retiree or a full-fledged one.

Keep a journal to record your own thoughts and questions about all the different sections of this book. Add your own insights and revelations, and use it to motivate yourself to start acting on your intentions. At the beginning of many sections, you'll find a quote. Ask yourself what message the quote has for you personally. Think of the quotes as words of wisdom given to you from across the ages. You'll also find quotes from ordinary people that I think you'll find just as meaningful as those from the great masters.

Use the quotes as springboards to come up with your own thoughts on the topics. You may want to write about the quotes in your journal or discuss them with a friend.

At the conclusion of each section, you'll find Takeaways, a summary of all the main points covered. These reviews will help reinforce your motivation to practice the suggestions offered throughout the book.

After some sections, you'll see a quiz. Don't worry. It's totally unlike those pesky ones you took in school that bamboozled you with choices like "all of the above" or "none of the above." Instead, these quizzes will test your knowledge of the many things listed in this book that you can do to make your retirement the best it can possibly be. As a bonus, they'll make you smile.

You can read the book consecutively or skip around, using your concerns on any given day as a guideline. Suppose you'd like to create a diet/exercise plan that you could stick with: read the section on health. Would you like to get more out of your love relationship? See the chapter entitled "Nurture Your Relationships." Are you growing apart from some of your old friends and wondering if you should continue these friendships or look for new ones? A segment in Chapter Three, "Expand Your Mind," can help you sort out this question.

Of course, I don't have all the answers about what will make everything fall into place for you or what will make you experience your own best version of the good life. But from one woman to another, I can promise you that I'm with you on every step of your journey.

Over the years, I've asked myself questions this book addresses, and I discover new questions and answers every day. One thing I do know is that I'm living the life I want to live, and you can too. Wouldn't it be amazing if you could start right now?

Chapter 1: Plan Your Future

1. Brainstorm Your Best Ideas

"To accomplish great things, we must not only act, but also dream, not only plan, but also believe."—Anatole France

Many people believe that we as women are more right-brained and intuitive than men. Although controversy abounds on this issue, a lot of us find this to be true. We wonder whether we're programmed that way or if it's the result of cultural conditioning. That said, many of us feel at ease using our right brains to help us find creative solutions to our problems.

When we activate our right brains, we surprise ourselves by coming up with exciting options that we'd never imagine ourselves having. Go ahead. Think of something you've always wanted to do but never dared try. How can you find a way to do it now? How will you begin this process that will set you on your way to living your best life now?

You'll probably want to start thinking six months to a few years before you retire about how you'd most like to spend your time. Record your thoughts in your journal on a regular basis on a certain day each week about how you'd like to see your retirement years playing out. Brainstorm with yourself. Jot down ideas in short snippets without thinking too much even if some of your ideas seem off-the-wall and outrageous. Let your right brain rule. For once, forget about the logic of your ideas.

You may also want to brainstorm with the family member or friend who knows you better than anyone else does. Two of you, totally in sync and thinking together, will come up with even more exciting ways to help plan your future.

Try brainstorming yourself and with a partner. See where it leads you.

2. Prioritize Your Thoughts

You'll be surprised by how many creative ideas your mind generates (even more if you're brainstorming with a friend). Your thoughts will flow easily, as never before. Next, take a moment to omit the ideas you know you won't use. Finally, arrange your ideas in order of how important they are to you. Juggle the numbers if you're writing; cut and paste if you're working on a computer.

Do this exercise as many times as you want. Don't judge; just write. Use sentences or phrases, whatever is easier for you. By the time you're ready to retire, you'll be closer to mapping out an individualized plan for yourself, making the coming years the best you could imagine. Now it's time to congratulate yourself for taking the first step. You're on your way to creating a vibrant, exciting life, one that will surpass your most improbable dreams.

3. Believe It Can Happen

"The future belongs to those who believe in the beauty of their dreams."—Eleanor Roosevelt

Picture yourself in all the different situations you've listed above. How would each of these scenarios make you feel? If you answered, *excited, rejuvenated, turned on, fired up,* or any words that mean absolute bliss to you, it's something you'll definitely want on your "to do" list.

Run your ideas by friends. See if they've ever thought seriously about pursuing their own dreams in retirement. What did they do to realize them? If not, what stopped them?

In the end, however, it's your call. Ask yourself what you'd like to do more than anything in the world and what you'll need to do to motivate yourself to get there. Take small steps. No pressure!

Believe it can happen, feel it in the core of your being. Then take the steps to make it a reality. And there's a good chance it will become a reality.

Picture yourself as a strong, confident woman who can achieve every goal you set for yourself. Begin today.

4. Figure Out Your Finances

"The only way to not think about money is to have a great deal of it."—Edith Wharton

As women, we're often the ones who budget, pay the bills, and handle the finances in our families. Planning for retirement may seem intimidating, but you've prepared for it all your life by being money conscious and consumer savvy. After all, who knows where to look for the best bargains?

How much money will you need to accomplish all the things you want to do when you retire? Will you have to take a part-time job to supplement your savings or investments? Figure out exactly how much money you have and a good estimate of what you will need to retire within your best comfort level. Leave some leeway for unexpected emergencies. Assess the state of your finances, and then come up with a plan.

How would you feel about skimping on certain things like eating out or buying a new wardrobe every season? Would it bother you if you had to cut back on gifts for family or friends? If you find your income reduced, you may want to figure out some realistic ways to bring in more funds to finance what's important to you.

If you think you need help from a professional, talk to a financial planner and come up with a plan that will keep you afloat financially and allow you to realize the freedom to live a life you'll love.

5. Dream Up Ways to Generate Money

"When I was young, I thought that money was the most important thing in life. Now that I am old, I know that it is."—Oscar Wilde

We, as women, know how to find answers for most problems we face in life. When your partner grappled with health or employment issues, you turned into "Dear Abby." If your kids had a conflict at school, you found an effective way to address it. Why should figuring out how to bring in more money in retirement be any different?

Talk to friends and family members to get ideas about how to bring in money if you need it. Look for part time jobs on the Internet and in the newspaper. If you need to supplement your income, find something you'll enjoy doing. For the second half of your life, allow yourself to make a different set of rules: guidelines you may not have thought about following before.

6. Think in New Ways About Jobs

Maybe you've worked in a job all your life because it brought you both money and satisfaction. Or maybe your job brought you a paycheck but little fulfillment. Whatever your circumstances now, consider this as your last best chance to choose a job on your own terms.

I recently met Dr. Beth, a retired physician who works as a shoe salesperson in a discount department store in Florida. She told me about her contentment in her new job of helping customers choose comfortable shoes at a fair price.

At the end of the day, Dr. Beth says she's tired but happy. She now goes home and forgets about her job. She no longer has to worry if she prescribed the best possible medicine for a patient's illness or if her patients will survive and thrive. Like many other women, Dr. Beth searched for a totally different type of job during her retirement that would help her use her people skills in a completely different way.

Think about doing only what you love, even if it brings in a little less money or seems like a job you wouldn't have taken before because it didn't match your educational background or qualifications.

You may also want to consider bartering your services with friends and acquaintances. If you don't need steady money coming in, bartering may offer a flexible solution. For example, if you're a teacher, offer to tutor your neighbors' kids, and they'll do basic repairs for you. Figure out a creative plan that works for you, and start implementing it. The possibilities are endless. Think of what you do well and what you don't like to do, and see if you can exchange these jobs with someone you know.

7. Write Your Future in the Present

"I am tomorrow, or some future day, what I establish today. I am today what I established yesterday or some previous day."—James Joyce

We know the importance of living in the moment. Often, when we think too far ahead, we miss out on the joys of the moment. Try projecting your thoughts into the future while acting as if that future is happening now. This exercise can help you picture what your life could be like if you'd allow yourself to grasp beyond what you've thought of as your reach.

If you try this exercise, I promise that you'll gain new insights into what your future could be like if you allow yourself to picture it as if it's happening this very moment. Imagine yourself five years from now. Write a story about what you'll be doing five years after you retire. Craft your story as if it's happening today. Use your five senses so that you actually feel your fantasies morphing into reality.

Think about a lifelong goal, dream job, or hobby you'd like to try. Imagine what it would feel like to finally get that degree, to sell one of your paintings, or to write a book (self or traditionally published) on a topic that intrigues you. Maybe you'd like to further your education or open a business. Nothing is beyond your reach.

8. Envision Your Future Now

Many of us find it hard to live in the moment. All our lives we've been asking questions like these: Is it going to work out with the person I love?; Am I going to get that promotion/raise?; or Will my kids get into the college they choose? In thinking ahead, we sometimes lost sight of the moment.

However, as we grow older, we become more aware of the rewards of being present in the moment. In this exercise you'll project your thoughts into the future, but you'll pretend it's the present. All you have to do is daydream about a future event as if you're actually there now experiencing it. Try it. What would your best life look like if you were experiencing it now?

Picture yourself in your favorite future scenario. See it, hear it, and feel it. Taste the buttery lobster and tart lemon pie you'll eat at your congratulatory dinner with family and friends.

Hear the words, "I'm so proud and happy for you" from those whose opinions matter most. Feel the warmth and support of your friends and family surrounding you and cheering you on for your accomplishment. Then do everything it takes to transport yourself to where you want to go.

9. Use Your Story to Guide Your Life

"Every great dream begins with a dreamer. Always remember, you have within you the strength, the patience, and the passion to reach for the stars, to change the world."—Harriet Tubman

Many women don't allow themselves to dream big. Some may view doing the preceding exercises as entertaining impractical fantasies that will never materialize. If you want the vision of your future to become a reality, you'll need to take the next step. You'll have to make your vision part of your life by using fantasizing as a tool to transport you to your goal.

Initially, it's okay for your vision to be fanciful and off-the-wall. You can always bring it down a notch. Your image of the future may not play out exactly as you'd like it, but aim high. Once you set the bar too low, it's hard to move it up. If you start with high hopes, you can always adjust them to your comfort level.

After you've written your story, look back at it every week and ask yourself if you're starting to make it your life story. If your plan isn't moving the way you want it, write down the specific things you'll do to make the things you want come into your life. Break down each goal you set into manageable steps. Check off each step as you take it. Above all, think of this as more than a story about your future. This is the rest of your life in the making. Don't wait.

10. Allow Yourself to Dream

Can you give yourself permission to dream? As women, we're often caught up in doing for others in our roles as mothers, spouses, and caregivers. Sometimes we mistakenly consider ourselves selfish if we spend time thinking about our own needs.

Think of a time when you asked yourself: What would it be like if I could have any job in the world, live any place in the world, and find what makes me happiest and do it?

When you allowed yourself to dream, what did it feel like? Did it make you feel more uplifted because you considered it possible or let down because you didn't think it could happen? Did you feel that some of your dreams were within reach, or did you see them as totally unattainable?

What if you started thinking about what might happen if you spent more time entertaining the fascinating possibilities that present themselves, sometime serendipitously, in your life? Are you open to saying it's all right to dream? Are you willing to see where your dreams will take you?

When I was a child, Mom and I played a game called "Make Believe and Then You Really." If we couldn't sleep, we'd close our eyes and pretend we were sleeping. Before we knew it, we'd drift into a deep, restful sleep. We'd wake up in the morning refreshed, and say, "That was easy." Sometimes we'd use our game to try our dreams for the future on for size. Imagine the excitement we felt when they'd sometimes come true.

Allow yourself to dream, and tell yourself that you will take steps to make your dreams materialize, no matter how far-fetched they seem. Try it. There's a good chance you'll be pleasantly surprised.

11. Pick a Day, An Ordinary Day

"To live is so startling it leaves little time for anything else."—Emily Dickenson

Do you remember the Thornton Wilder play, "Our Town"? Emily, a young mother who dies in childbirth, gets one chance to relive any day in her life. She could have chosen the day she graduated from high school or her wedding day. Instead, she chose her 12th birthday.

She begins to relive the day, but she can't bear the pain associated with it. She concludes that people should value life "every, every minute." When she asks the stage manager/narrator if people realize the beauty of life as they live it, he responds, "No. The saints and poets, maybe—they do some..."

This scene brings home the fact that the ordinary days often resonate more with us than the big days. Maybe it's because these seemingly insignificant events trigger the deep emotional connections we share with those we love best: our mates, parents, brothers, sisters, grandparents, and all those closest to us.

By remembering ordinary days and events, we begin to see what's truly important to us: a loving touch, a moment of mutual understanding, or a shared experience that helps both people appreciate what's truly important.

Try to think of all these things as you write in the present tense about the past. In your journal, describe an ordinary day you spent with a cherished relative when you were growing up. Describe what you and your family member did that day that made it extraordinary although back then it seemed like a regular day. Recall exactly what it felt like: what you saw, heard, smelled, or tasted. Write your story as if it's happening now.

12. Bring That Day to Life

Think back to when you were a child. What was it about that day that made it stand out in your memory? What was it about that experience that you crave in your life now? Was it how special you felt when your dad spent the morning planting flowers with you? Was it the scent of those roses that still bloom even though other people live in your childhood home these days?

Maybe the anticipation of the special dinner your mother always cooked on your birthday brings a special day to mind. Do you recall how you could request anything you wanted, from the fried chicken and corn on the cob to the crunchy ice cream cake?

Stop for a moment. Remember that day and, as you relive it, you'll begin to feel that you're actually there. What could make you experience these feelings now? What if you could feel that way again? Strive to bring experiences into your life that generate these simple yet sublimely joyful feelings.

Chapter 1. Takeaways

- Brainstorm your possibilities.
- Map out a precise plan for your future.
- Believe your plan will happen.
- Design a financial plan.
- Discover ways to make extra money.
- Rethink job options.
- Imagine yourself in the future now.
- Create a future success scene.
- Aim high, dream big.
- Give yourself permission to dream.
- Capture the magic in the ordinary.
- Experience feelings that bring you joy.

Quiz #1: Plan Your Future

Now it's time for a quiz on everything we've discussed in Chapter One. No pressure—no stress. Have fun with it, and use the easy self-scoring guide to analyze your score in this and the quizzes that follow.

Are you doing all you can do to plan for your future? Take the quiz and find out.

1. When thinking about what you'd like to do when you retire, it's best to

   a) wait until you retire. You'll have oodles of time to decide then.
   b) let your right brain jumpstart your creative powers.
   c) let your logical brain rule and plan things to a tea.

2. What will help you decide on some definite goals for retirement?

   a) Writing down all my ideas, putting them in a hat, and choosing a few with eyes shut
   b) Whether the ideas I chose excite me and make me happy
   c) Visiting the senior center and talking to the members as they slurp coffee and devour donuts

3. What do you need to consider when assessing your finances for retirement?

   a) What your chances are of winning the lottery or making it big in a second career
   b) Whether to take a part-time job and how you'd feel about cutting back
   c) Whether you should think twice about retiring now

4. What is the most important thing to consider when thinking of ways to generate money during retirement?

    a) Find a job that matches your educational credentials. You wouldn't want to take a step down—would you?

    b) Think about doing only what you love.

    c) Take the job that gives you the most money. Why settle for less?

5. What's the best way to help you write your story about realizing your future dreams?

    a) Write it like it's a fairy tale because it may not happen, and you don't want to be disappointed.

    b) Write your story as if it's happening now.

    c) Write it in the future tense as if you're looking forward to that day.

6. What will you do if your future story isn't unfolding as you planned?

    a) Modify your goals. Maybe you're thinking too big.

    b) Write the steps you'll take to make each goal come into your life.

    c) Chalk it off to reality, and think about being more practical.

7. What will reliving a happy day from the past help you do?

    a) Drive home the stark reality that your best days are behind you

    b) Make you think about the experiences that you want in your life now

    c) Remind you that it's time to concentrate on the future and forget about the past

Answers

Mostly A's: It matters how you think, and it definitely influences the way your retirement years will pan out for you. Chill out, don't fret, and allow yourself to dream. You'll see that it's fun to take a chance and to break the mold you've been in for too long. Do it now.

Mostly B's: You're on your way to creating an adventurous retirement for yourself. You're practical without being stuffy and realistic without being boring and predictable. You're on your way to realizing your dreams.

Mostly C's: You've got a practical side—and that's good. However, give yourself permission to think in new ways to open up more possibilities for your future. Let down your hair. Think in ways you never had the freedom to think before. Have fun and entertain your dreams.

Chapter 2: Boost Your Physical and Emotional Health

13. Organize Your Day

"Organize your life around your dreams—and watch them come true." —Unknown

We have always had to juggle responsibilities like jobs, spouses, kids, and chores. We're experts at keeping to-do lists and carrying them out to the letter. Rest assured that your experience with organizational skills will greatly benefit you in retirement.

Even if you've never done it before, keep a record of what you have to do each day. Giving structure to your day will make setting goals easier and help you embrace a sense of purpose in your life.

Think about this: Are there some chores you've disliked all your life, such as cleaning, cooking, or coloring your hair? If you're not hurting for money, consider hiring someone to clean and cook. If money's tight, you and a friend can work together to clean, exchange meals, or color one another's hair. You're not bound to distasteful jobs forever if you're willing to look for creative alternatives.

Plan tasks for the next day the night before. Include routine jobs like bills, clean up/fix up projects, and errands. But also list hobbies, activities (Chapter Five gives you options for hobbies and activities) and second career aspirations you love but never had time to pursue. Pencil in things you enjoy just as you schedule chores and errands. Which phase of one of your pet projects will you work on tomorrow to bring you closer to accomplishing it?

14. Keep a Job Log

Are you ready to start organizing your life? Record your job log in a small notebook rather than on little pieces of paper that will scatter all over your desk and disappear. Cross off the jobs as you do them. Think of your special projects and hobbies as jobs you want to accomplish. You'll be more likely to accomplish them.

The next day, flip back to see if you've neglected anything on your list. Keeping this log will help you see you're accomplishing something each day, and that's wiser than leaving it all to chance.

You may also want to keep a mini notebook in your purse to record ideas about creative things you want to do or any thoughts you have that you don't want to slip by you. Keep phone numbers and e-mail addresses of interesting people you meet along the way in a separate section of your notebook. If you come across an intriguing site or restaurant you'd like to visit, note that too, and make it a point to go there.

Speaking of purses, do you ever have trouble finding your cell phone, keys, or a certain credit card? Look for one of those purses that have different compartments sewn in the bottom, where each one of your necessities will find a separate, secure home. Best of all, no more fumbling. Many companies make them, and you can find one at a fair price.

15. Eat to Live

"One should eat to live, not live to eat."—Moliere

You'll find plenty of temptations in retirement, and food is a major one. Everywhere you look you'll find it: from the goodies at the local coffee shop (you can't have coffee without a donut) to your own refrigerator and pantry, which now seem stuffed with all the foods you've always loved but didn't have time to think about when you were working or carpooling the kids.

Another obstacle to keeping slim and trim is that we're free to grab a snack anytime we want. At work, you may have felt awkward if you'd pigged out with big portions of decadent delights in full view of your co-workers. At home, who's going to see if you polish off that oversized wedge of fudge cake or dig into Whoopie Cookie ice cream straight from the carton?

16. Find a Sensible Approach to Eating

You've heard that we sometimes gain weight during retirement because we're at the age where our bodies put on pounds faster. If you want to lose weight and keep it off, start by picturing yourself with the svelte, healthy body you've always wanted.

The worst thing you can do as you grow older is overeat, not only because of menacing health problems like high blood pressure and cholesterol, but also because you want to feel energized and look like the foxy mama you are.

If you'd like a program that doesn't require you to figure out a diet plan yourself, join a group plan that helps you calculate calories and offers choices. Plans like this also offer motivation if you find other people's support helpful. On the other hand, a plan that features packaged meals might also appeal to you if you don't feel like counting calories or measuring portions.

Whatever you decide, make a strong effort to fill your fridge with healthy foods. If you feel that you need to eat between meals, chose healthy snacks. You don't have to deprive yourself totally of the sweets, treats, and dishes you love; all you need to do is eat them sensibly. Make an eating plan that's workable for you, and stick with it.

17. Devise an Individual Eating Plan

"Eat what you want. Just don't eat too much of any one thing."
—My mom

If you're a person who would rather lose weight on your own, try cutting calories in a reasonable way and increasing your exercise. Find a calorie chart, keep a record of what you eat, and don't exceed your target calorie count. Be sure to measure portions.

On the other hand, some women find that weighing what they eat discourages them from implementing their weight loss program. If so, don't use a food scale. Just use your best judgment and measure out a reasonable portion. Or use one of the sample portion systems that you can easily find online, calling for a handful, fistful, etc., of the food you want to eat.

You'll also want to add more healthy foods (grains, vegetables, fruits, and yogurt, for example) to your diet and to cut back on fried and fatty foods. That is not to say you can never eat the foods you love. Just have some of these forbidden foods occasionally, or cut back on how much of them you eat. Love butter but hate the fat? Add a smidgeon, not a glob, to your baked potato. Do you dream about ice cream? Reach for a low cal version or eat half as much as you usually do.

You may drop pounds more slowly, but if being in total control of your plan works for you, that's the way to go. Set a weight and size goal for yourself, and create a diet plan that's custom made for you.

Whatever plan you choose, losing weight with a friend will make it easier. Call or visit one another to talk about your progress. Reward yourselves with lunch (low cal, of course) when you see results.

18. Exercise to Your Own Beat

"Anyone's life truly lived consists of work, sunshine, exercise, soap, plenty of fresh air, and a happy contented spirit." —Lily Langtree

Many fitness centers will give you a free trial. Take advantage of it so that you can see which exercise excites you without first spending a lot of money.

What kind of exercise turns you on? Do you enjoy hopping on an indoor bike or a treadmill with your headset on, listening to music, or watching an exercise video on TV? Maybe you'd prefer riding your bike in the park or around your neighborhood. On the other hand, maybe you love to dance. You could try Zumba or jazz dancing with a group.

If you want to keep up with an exercise program, you have to choose one you love and commit to doing it regularly (3-5 times a week). If you find it hard to get out of bed to make it to your class on time, set the clock a little earlier so you won't feel harried. Take the time to have a light snack and some juice an hour or so before your class. Set out your exercise clothes the night before to streamline your preparation in the morning.

Being with other women will inspire you to keep moving to the beat. You'll be surprised at how the exercise you choose will slim your waistline and give you rock solid abs—if you do it regularly. Try it for a month and see the difference.

Best of all, your heart and digestive systems will thank you. Your body seems to work better when you exercise regularly. Your brain will also reward you by coming up with more creative and exciting ideas. Further, you're likely to build up better immunity and catch fewer colds and flu bugs.

19. Get Up and Go, Go, Go

To motivate yourself to get in shape, shop for exercise outfits in colors you love, along with a comfortable pair of sneakers geared to the type of exercise you're doing. If you're running, you'll want running shoes; if you're doing aerobics, look for cross trainers. If you're a Zumba fan, you may want to buy Zumba shoes so you won't fall when you spin around. However, sneakers will work just as well for most people.

One thing you'll want to spend time looking for is a comfortable sports bra that fits just right. Many of them squeeze you in, and others that offer little support cause you to flop and sag, an uncomfortable feeling, to say the least. Check out some styles in stores and online that suit your fancy.

Don't forget colorful headbands to keep your hair out of your eyes. (I like the skinny elastic ones that come in a bunch of colors that you can buy in a discount store.) A spiffy water bottle will help keep you hydrated.

Put on your new workout clothes and running shoes and prepare to look and feel like a new woman, one who's fired up and raring to go. Once you start, you won't want to stop. Trust me.

20. Keep Moving

"All truly great thoughts are conceived by walking."—*Frederic Nietzsche*

You're probably thinking that it's not enough to embark on an exercise program if you want to keep in tip-top shape. You're right. Make keeping active a way of life if you want to look and feel in top form every day. There are many things you can do to boost your stamina and positive outlook.

In addition to the old standbys of parking a little farther from the grocery store or taking the stairs instead of the elevator, add a walking or biking program to your regular exercise routine. You'll burn off more calories and increase your stamina and energy level.

Is your hobby or new career based on sitting at your computer? Every hour or so, get up and move around. Put on music and dance to a couple of songs you love. Dig into a chore like cleaning out your bookshelf or gathering clothes that you no longer wear to donate to a worthy cause.

Move your body intermittently between engaging in sedentary activities like computer work, reading, or crafting. You'll be surprised at how doing these small physical chores and adding a walking or biking program will complement your exercise program in keeping you fit in mind and body. Take it from me—you'll feel more alive than you did when you were younger.

Keep moving!

21. Treat Yourself Kindly

Many women feel more comfortable carrying a few extra pounds, and heredity predisposes others to have more full-figured bodies.

Let me ask you this: What are your thoughts about this discussion about diets and exercise? If you're happy with your body image exactly the way it is, that's fine. If you've tried diets and exercise and nothing seems to work, unless you're at the point where your weight compromises your health, accept and respect yourself for who you are. Expect the same treatment from others. People may voice their concerns about your health, but that doesn't give anyone the right to judge you.

By the same token, it doesn't hurt to give thought to eating healthy foods and to find an exercise you like to stay fit. However, we all know that some people find it hard, if not impossible, to shed pounds. Given these obstacles, think about whether it's a good idea for you to try. If you choose to start a diet and exercise program, be kind and loving to yourself, just as you'd be to a friend who wasn't getting results as quickly as she wanted.

22. Carry Yourself with Confidence

"Look at me, girl. I'm getting sexier every day, and I'm loving it: curvy hips, ample bosoms, and shapely legs—who could ask for more? If you've got it, flaunt it."—Older woman remarking to her grown daughter while trying on dresses in the plus-size department

Women often judge themselves harshly when it comes to body image. Magazines, movies, and TV tout extreme thinness as the ideal shape, but we've learned that some of these models suffer from eating disorders. Many stores promote skinny jeans and skimpy bathing suits, but how many women can actually wear them?

It's important to love your body, whatever shape you're in. We can still look attractive if we carry a few extra pounds. If you walk and talk confidently and act as if you're proud of who you are, people will perceive you that way. You have to be the one who decides whether to lose weight or to stay exactly the way you are.

Consider health factors, but after you tally that in, appreciate your body image and move like you believe it. Then you and everyone else will see you for what you are—beautiful in body and spirit.

23. Put on Your Best Face

Mom always said, "Before you go out, wash your face, brush your teeth, comb your hair, and slap on a little make-up."

One seemingly simple thought about personal appearance struck me shortly after I retired. Every day before going to my job, I took time to be sure my clothes, make-up, and hair looked stylish. I found that the effort was well worth it because it was part of the professional image I needed to project to gain my students' respect.

Appearance on the job can make or break an employee because it can greatly affect a person's image with supervisors and co-workers. After retiring, I started wearing more casual, comfortable clothes but soon found that I missed dressing up. My friend said that even though she works at her computer from home most days, she feels much better when she takes the time to dress in casual yet stylish clothes.

After we retire, we're used to flying out of the house without taking the time to look our best, and that's exactly the day we'll run into someone we know. You could try to hide between the clothes racks or make a mad dash from the dairy aisle to the seafood counter. But there's an easier way.

We all know that when we look better we feel more upbeat and optimistic. And how long does it take to slather on some moisturizer, dab on a little foundation and blush, and comb our hair a little? You can pop on a funky fedora or a jazzy headband if you're having a bad hair day.

Once you get started, you may not want to stop with your face and hair. If you're going to all that trouble, why not trade your sweatpants and hoodie for a comfortable pair of pants, a colorful top, and a snappy jacket? Don't forget a patterned scarf. If you like sneakers, find a pretty pair to complement your outfit.

Try trading your casual look for a new look for a week, and see what happens.

24. Take the Time to Care About Your Appearance

"Vanity of vanities...All is vanity."— *Ecclesiastes 1:2*

Does it mean we're vain if we care about our appearance? How do you feel about that? Personally, I think it shows we care enough about ourselves to look our best for our own sakes. Another benefit to this quick beauty routine is that it may preserve our skin better because of the skin protection in the products.

Why blend in with the crowd when you can stand out and make a statement about who you are? Although how you act and what you do speak more for you than your appearance, it's an important part of who you are and the image you choose to project to yourself and others.

Some women may opt for cosmetic surgery, and that's a viable choice if they want it. But you can easily enhance your appearance with cosmetics and an inexpensive wardrobe makeover.

You're probably wondering whether I'd advise a man to take the time to give attention to his appearance and look his best. The answer is *yes* because our appearance is closely tied in with how we feel about ourselves and how we want others to perceive us. It's important to look and feel your best today. Do you have a few minutes to spare?

25. Sleep to Restore Yourself

"O, Sleep, O Gentle Sleep, nature's soft nurse..."
—*Henry IV, Shakespeare*

It's hard to believe that you have fewer hours in the day now than when you held down a full time job and tended to the endless tasks you had to do. You may find yourself so busy now that getting to sleep and staying asleep requires more effort.

Although it's not always easy, you'll feel better if you go to sleep and wake up around the same time each day. Unless you're planning a romantic evening, try to wind down gradually before you hit the pillow to prepare your mind and body for a restful sleep.

Talk to friends your age, and you'll find that many of them have sleeping problems. Ask what they do, and see if it might work for you. As we grow older, we often require less sleep, but it's important to get high quality sleep. Be careful with over-the-counter sleep preparations, and be fully aware of side effects. If you have serious problems snoozing, talk to your doctor and work toward a solution that's right for you.

26. Don't Just Lie There—Do Something

Why do so many retired women have trouble sleeping? While hormonal fluctuations may cause some sleeping disorders, sometimes the lack of routine or worries about health, family, or finances can precipitate sleeping woes. Suppose you can't sleep even after you've tried everything? Don't upset yourself further by lying in bed staring at the dark ceiling. Go to another room, read a book, work on a puzzle, or catch up on light chores. Avoid using your computer because you may become keyed up.

Once you feel sleepy (and this is important—be sure you're

sleepy enough), grab your pillow and settle comfortably under the covers. Here's another simple thing you can do to prepare for sleep when cold weather hits: warm your pj's or nightgown in the dryer for a few minutes. You'll be surprised by how cozy and relaxed that can make you feel. You can also try wearing socks when it's chilly; if your feet feel warm, your whole body will rest easier.

If you're tired during the day from not sleeping, you may want to take a nap, and that's okay. However, be sure you don't nap too long or you won't sleep at night. Figure out by experimenting whether a nap would enhance or impede your sense of restfulness.

If your sleeplessness intensifies, talk to your doctor and explain your specific sleep problem. Do you have trouble falling asleep, or do you wake sometime during the night and have a hard time getting back to sleep? Is your sleep problem chronic, or does it happen only occasionally? Before resorting to a sleeping medication, consult with your physician to see whether one would help you on a short-term basis. Do everything you can to help yourself before taking over-the-counter or prescription medicines since many of these preparations can cause side effects, some of them serious. You also may want to investigate natural sleep aids sold in health food stores.

You deserve restful sleep. Do whatever it takes to get it.

27. Resolve to Stop Smoking

"Giving up smoking is the easiest thing in the world. I know because I've done it thousands of times." —Mark Twain

If you're a smoker, begin a plan to stop smoking now. You know that smoking can cause serious lung problems and precipitates many types of cancer. And if you're concerned about looking the best you can at any age, smoking can bring on wrinkles and make you age quickly.

In our mothers' generation, and even when we were younger, many women smoked because they thought smoking made them look provocative and sophisticated. On TV and in the movies, someone was always lighting up, thinking she looked glamorous. Now women say they smoke because it helps relieve stress. But you can find much better tension busters than cigarettes.

Some women smoke because they say it keeps excess pounds from piling up. But what good is that if it makes you look and feel older? Many women who smoke are more prone to skin wrinkling and sagging. Sure, it's hard to stop smoking, but talk to your doctor about different plans, and pick the one you think will work best for you.

You don't want to smell like tobacco breath or to hurt the people around you by polluting their world with smoke. Now is the time to quit.

28. Think When You Drink

"Drunkenness is simply voluntary insanity."—Seneca

There's certainly nothing wrong with having a little wine with your dinner, but everyone knows it's best not to overindulge in alcohol. We're so used to drinking socially that we often don't think about the downside of using alcohol. The worst problem, of course, comes when people drive after drinking. With you, that could mean after one or after three drinks. Only you know how much alcohol you can handle.

So, if you enjoy a drink now and then, by all means, have it. However, as our bodies change, our tolerance levels for alcohol and medications may also change. Consider this if you drink.

The truth is that sometimes people with more time on their hands or those who are going through a major change in lifestyle may be more likely to turn to alcohol to help them cope with the many transitions they're facing. The bottom line is to be sure you're not drinking to ease loneliness, boredom, frustration, or depression. It pays to think when you drink.

29. Use Prescription Drugs Wisely

"The art of medicine consists in amusing the patient while nature cures the disease."—Voltaire

By the time we reach a certain age, most of us take one or more prescription medicines. Many people also take drugs for mental health problems, particularly depression. In line with this, be sure your doctor evaluates you for underlying physical problems before prescribing drugs for mental health issues.

Unfortunately, a few medical practitioners still believe in the stereotype of the "hysterical female" and quickly prescribe anti-anxiety and anti depressive medications without fully researching a woman's symptoms. Also, due to research findings, many doctors advise stopping hormone replacement therapy and instead recommend antidepressants to take the edge off menopausal symptoms that can last for years.

Sometimes, however, doing this exchanges one set of problems for another, as many antidepressants carry serious side effects. If your symptoms persist and you don't want to take hormone replacement therapy for any length of time, discuss natural preparations, along with a stress reduction and exercise program, with your medical practitioner.

Ask yourself if the drugs you are taking are enhancing your life or hurting it. If you feel that the drugs you are taking are harming you physically or emotionally, talk with your doctor about reevaluating your need for them or about changing your prescriptions.

30. Research Your Meds

In our parents' day, many women accepted their physicians' advice without questioning them or doing their own independent research. Now we feel free to ask about the advisability of choosing one drug over another and to question doctors about the drug's positive and negative attributes.

Take the time to research side effects and long-term consequences of the drugs you're taking. Look at the drug companies' websites to view potential side effects, keeping in mind that very few people may experience some of the negative effects listed. However, if you feel uncomfortable about taking the drug after reading what the websites say, ask for a substitute.

Related to this is that reading customer reviews about drugs and lifesaving medical procedures, that some of us avoid because of fear, can cause us deep emotional distress. One person's experiences with a drug or procedure may differ markedly from another's. Sometimes studying these reviews can steer us away from a lifesaving drug or procedure. If you read reviews, keep an open mind toward them and then decide how to proceed.

You'll also want to talk to your pharmacist about medicines. Due to extensive training, pharmacists usually have an excellent understanding of how drugs affect us, and they're often willing to spend the time discussing it. Be sure your prescription drugs enhance your quality of life, rather than worsen it.

Chapter 2: Takeaways

- Give structure to your day.

- Think of your projects and hobbies as jobs.

- Don't deprive yourself when dieting, but eat sensibly.

- Create a diet plan that's right for you.

- Choose an exercise plan you love and commit to it.

- Push yourself to keep moving throughout the day.

- Appreciate your body image, and move as if you believe it.

- Take steps to keep up your appearance.

- Tackle sleep problems creatively.

- Resolve to stop smoking.

- Drink responsibly.

- Evaluate your use of prescription drugs.

Chapter 3: Expand Your Mind

31. Interact with Your Books

*"One must be an inventor in order to read well.
There is then creative reading as well as creative
writing."—Ralph Waldo Emerson*

Physical exercise can add quality years to your life. And so can the quiet time you spend reading and reflecting on what you've read. When you take the time to expand your mind by interacting with your books, it can heighten your reading pleasure. How can you do this? It's easy. When you read, stop every so often and think about what you've read. Keep a notebook to record powerful thoughts and quotes or record them in a section of your journal.

Write down issues the book brings to mind that you'd like to explore by yourself or in conversations with friends. You can also jot down vocabulary words to look up or references you'd like to explore.

Call me a nerd, but I've discovered more reading pleasure by perusing bibliographies in favorite books and then discovering even more fascinating books on the topic. See how much knowledge you can squeeze out of one book by reading it to the very last page.

32. Ask Questions As You Read

Ask yourself questions as you read: for example, if you were the author, how would you have handled the plot, theme, and characters of a fiction book? If you're reading non-fiction, do you agree or disagree with the author's advice? If you disagree, what would be your advice to readers?

Reading this way, instead of merely passively ingesting a

book's content and taking it at face value, will help unleash your own creativity in all areas of your life.

If you visit Facebook or other social media sites, post your reaction to something you've read. Start a discussion or even an argument. Keep the juices flowing. Talk to your books, and your books will talk back to you.

33. Go Within

"Meditation brings wisdom; lack of meditation leaves ignorance. Know well what leads you forward and what holds you back, and choose the path that leads to wisdom."—Buddha

Have you ever thought about practicing some form of meditation? It can give you a quick pick-me-up when you're fighting fatigue or not feeling your best.

Meditation helps you relate better to people and to tone down your anger and stress buttons. You'll be less apt to react negatively when life deals you big and little irritations. Meditation also helps you become more creative in finding solutions to problems since it heightens your intuition and sense of right action.

Decision-making becomes more effortless, and you'll be more likely to find a prime parking space without circling the lot repeatedly. This form of relaxation also enhances thinking in new and different ways about your job and artistic pursuits.

To get started, choose a mantra (a word you'll use to help you relax), and start meditating. Use any word that you find appealing, like *flower* or *river*, or even a favorite color. If you want, make your mantra an appealing phrase or a short prayer.

When different thoughts intervene, especially if they're disturbing, don't pay attention to them. Don't try to force them out; just let them pass and view them neutrally. Shift gently back to your mantra.

34. Choose a Fitting Meditation

If you'd prefer, you can use your breathing, rather than a mantra, as a meditating tool. All you have to do is be conscious of breathing in and breathing out.

You can practice another type of meditation called Kirtan Krya by sitting or walking. It involves saying a mantra while touching each finger to the thumb and saying the mantra silently or aloud. You can google this type of meditation and even watch a youtube.com video that will tell you exactly how to do it. If you're a person who likes to feel you're actively doing something and moving around rather than sitting still, you may prefer this type of meditation.

Whatever type of meditation you choose (mantra, moving, or breathing), about five minutes before your session ends, stop saying the mantra or being conscious of your breathing. To help time yourself, peek at a clock every so often. Simply sit there and relax to end your session.

You can do a mini meditation for a couple of minutes one or more times a day, or you can meditate for two twenty minute sessions. Either way, you'll come away relaxed and energized. You'll also become more calm and creative. And it's free for the asking.

35. Be Here Now

"You must live in the present, launch yourself on every wave, find your eternity in each moment. Fools stand on their island of opportunities and look toward another land. There is no other land; there is no other life but this."—Henry David Thoreau

Some people prefer meditating as they go about their daily tasks, such as dressing, cooking, walking, and creating. Mindfulness meditation asks you to be present and to think about what you're doing as you do it.

We live such hectic lives that our minds race ahead, and we miss out on the small moments that often bring us as much joy as the great events. Often we move robotically as if in a trance, so that we're not truly conscious of the happiness each moment holds.

When we drive, we sometimes wonder how we got from here to there because we're focusing on our destination and what we'll do when we arrive, rather than about the journey itself. Throughout the day we watch the clock, hoping that we'll quickly complete a task we don't enjoy so that we can race on to the next one. In doing this, we may miss out on the satisfaction of relishing a job and perceiving what we learn as we do it.

Be conscious of each moment and boost your happiness quotient.

36. Be Mindful in Everything You Do

When you eat, take a bath, or play a game outdoors with your grandchild or someone else, think about what you're doing each moment, and you'll experience simple pleasures as never before. These moments become extraordinary and make you feel that you're truly living your life rather than going through the motions without deeply feeling each experience.

For example, when you take a walk in the springtime, use all of your senses to revel in that walk. Smell the fragrant air, hear the birds singing, and touch that velvety pink rose petal. Everything in nature will seem much more alive to you.

As you bite into those creamy cheese potatoes you cooked for a special dinner or ate at your favorite restaurant, notice how the crusty cheddar complements the subtle blandness of the potato.

When you take a bath, observe that sudden rush of warmth as you lower your body into the tub. When you play catch with a child, feel the slap of the ball on your open palms, and listen to the upbeat exclamations of the child as she dives in to catch the ball.

Begin to feel more alive now. Perceive each moment as a gift and experience it as never before. Why wait?

37. Engage Your Brain

"I keep busy every minute. I don't let little annoyances like aches and pains keep me down. I'm constantly doing fun stuff, even when I'm here working."—Kimberly, 61-year-old waitress in the local diner in Savannah, Georgia, where they serve scrumptious mushroom omelets.

Once we retire, we're tempted to spend time relaxing and watching TV or frittering away precious hours on the phone or the Internet. However, most of us choose to keep our minds alive by making new friends, engaging in stimulating conversations, and finding hobbies and interests that distract us from whatever problems life deals us.

Once in a while, give yourself permission to indulge yourself, and don't let a guilty thought intrude if you feel like calling an old friend or checking your Facebook page. Sometimes watching your favorite TV program or a movie you've always wanted to see can lift your spirits if you're racing around and craving some down time with no worries and no responsibilities. For the most part, of course, you'll want to keep moving, thinking, and growing because you know that's what best for your body, mind, and spirit.

Did you ever think about how important it is to keep your brain juices flowing? Not only will it stave off physical problems, but it will also help counteract depression and degenerative diseases of the brain.

What kinds of things can you do to keep your brain active for as long as possible? As always, ask the questions: "What interests me most? What do I most enjoy doing?" As you've seen by now, that's the main mindset that will launch you on the path to success in your new life.

38. Keep Thinking and Growing

Some of us love verbal or math puzzles; others find them frustrating. We all know how important it is to read books, newspapers, and magazines to keep in touch with what's going on in the world. Discussing current affairs with friends and family members can also keep your brain nimble.

Reading and reflecting upon classic literature in prose or poetry (Shakespeare or the Romantic poets, for example) can teach you the wisdom of the ages. Spending time with children can give you fresh new insights on life you may not have considered.

Observe children's spontaneity as they throw themselves into each activity. Feel their excitement as they play a sport or a game. Like them, try to play more and worry less. Wordsworth said, "The child is father of the man." (I would add *woman*.) Sometimes we learn more about becoming totally immersed in a blissful life by watching children, than they can learn from watching us.

Find something that will totally engross you, and focus on it completely. It can be something simple like a scrambled word puzzle or something more complex like reading a challenging book or a type of book you haven't read before, or trying a new skill like playing a new sport or learning how to decorate cakes. Whatever you choose, throw yourself into your project to give your brain a rigorous workout.

Keep your brain busy. Your mind will thank you. And any physical ailments you have won't seem as alarming.

39. Balance Your Days

"The calm and balanced mind is the strong and great mind; the hurried and agitated mind is the weak one."—Wallace D. Wattles

Sometimes we get caught up in the grind of our daily lives—bill paying, home repairs, and shopping, and forget about aiming for balance. But that sense of balance is important because it's a main contributor to a sense of satisfaction and fulfillment for all of us. Make a conscious effort to balance the newfound solitude in your life with social activities.

Make time for yourself and what you love doing, but also spend time discussing important issues and concerns with friends and family members. As they help you by providing a sounding board for your ideas and dreams, you'll reciprocate by listening to them when they come to you for help or advice.

Spending too much solitary time can make you feel lonely, while spending most of your time going out to lunch, shows, or shopping with friends can make you lose sight of the goals you've set for yourself.

Figure out how you can adjust your time to make room for everything you want to do. You'll be surprised at how much more gratifying each day will become.

40. Find and Cultivate Friendships

"There is one friend in the life of each of us, who seems not a separate person, however dear and beloved, but an expansion, an interpretation, of one's self, the very meaning of one's soul."—Edith Wharton

Besides adding a sense of connection and warmth to your life, finding new friends and keeping in touch with longtime friends can help you stay active mentally. When you bounce ideas off one another and confide in each other, this give-and-take helps both your mind and your spirit. However, retirement often prompts people to reevaluate their friendships. Sometimes we lose touch with old friends and make new ones although there are always friends who will remain in our hearts and lives forever.

Do you find that you and some of your old friends don't have as much in common now that you're retired? Maybe it's because they're still working or caring for grandchildren.

Did you ever hear of someone going back to visit friends at work after they retired? Often, they'll tell you that it doesn't seem the same. They're still there doing the same thing, while you've come to a different place in your life. Because of that, it's sometimes harder to relate to one another.

Whatever the reason, this may mean cultivating some new friends. Of course, you'll stick with some of your old friends too. Some of the best friends we now have we've made in high school and college. But if you find some of your past friendships not as satisfying as they once were, it may be time to take another look at them.

You may also want to consider making friends with people in different age groups. Doing this can help you keep mentally active and, in turn, offer younger people the benefit of your experience and wisdom.

Surround yourself with friends of all ages, and you'll learn from each other and become more open to new ideas and a variety of opinions that you can discuss and debate. You and your younger friends won't always agree, but you'll enjoy the lively discussions. As an added perk, you'll take away a new perspective on current affairs and popular culture.

More often than not, however, some of our old friends provide us with anchors to the past and a feeling of security and comfort throughout our future. Remember the Girl Scout motto:

"Make new friends and keep the old; one is silver and the other is gold."

Whatever works for you is the right way to go.

Chapter 3: Takeaways

- Become an active reader.

- Decrease your stress level and boost your creativity by meditating.

- Be mindful of every moment.

- Engage your brain by doing what you love.

- Find unique ways to think and grow each day.

- Strive for balance in work, play, and private time.

- Nourish old friendships and seek out new ones.

Quiz #2: Boost Your Physical and Emotional Health and Expand Your Mind

Think about how your physical and emotional health affect your satisfaction in retirement. Consider how expanding your mind can help you grow more vibrant and alive. Based on what you've read in these chapters, choose the best answer from the choices given.

1. When you organize your day, how should you factor in your special projects and hobbies?

    a) As actual jobs
    b) As side interests that are not that important
    c) As luxuries you may never have time for

2. What is the best way to watch your weight?

   a) Eat sensibly, and don't totally deprive yourself of everything you love.
   b) Avoid eating between meals.
   c) Cut calories drastically if you want quick results. Show some discipline.

3. Which one tip can best help motivate you to reach your ideal weight?

   a) Plan to lose weight with a friend.
   b) Give yourself a tongue-lashing when you crave a hot fudge sundae.
   c) Pin up a picture of a rail-skinny model, and don't stop dieting until you become her clone.

4. What's the main thing to consider when choosing the exercise you'll do?

   a) Choose something you love.
   b) Choose something that makes you sweat profusely.
   c) Go to the gym with the best deal.

5. What can you do to keep active between sedentary activities?

   a) Dance or complete a chore.
   b) Take a stair-climbing break.
   c) Do rigorous sit-ups, push-ups, and crunches

6. What's a good reason to look your best every day?

   a) You'll feel more upbeat and optimistic.
   b) People will never guess how old you are.
   c) You can tell your friends to eat their hearts out.

7. What can you do to help you sleep better at night?

   a) Keep a regular schedule. Try to go to sleep and get up
      at the same time.
   b) Watch TV until you doze off.
   c) Count by 5s until you reach 200.

8. What is the most important reason to stop smoking?

   a) It can cause serious health problems.
   b) Tobacco breath turns people off.
   c) Smoking causes wrinkles and crows' feet.

9. It's never a good idea to drink if you're

   a) lonely or bored.
   b) celebrating with friends.
   c) going out with your puritanical relatives.

10. It's important to ask yourself if your prescription drugs are

   a) enhancing your life or hurting it.
   b) potent enough to work their magic.
   c) easy to swallow.

11. As you read a book, it can enhance your reading pleasure to

   a) stop periodically and think about what you've read.
   b) memorize a favorite passage.
   c) write a book report and show it to a friend.

12. What is the best aid to meditation?

   a) A mantra or breathing
   b) A dimly lit candle in a darkened room
   c) Sitting for an hour cross-legged on a fluffy pillow

13. Practicing mindfulness means

    a) becoming more aware of each moment.

    b) paying attention to every detail of your day.

    c) speaking your mind when someone aggravates you.

14. Spending time with children is a major way of

    a) keeping your mind active.

    b) learning cool slang.

    c) wearing yourself out.

15. Why is seeking balance in your life important?

    a) It can help you make time for everything you want to do.

    b) It can help you make time to see all your friends an equal amount of time.

    c) It can help you find time to do all the chores you've put off for years.

16. Why should you think about keeping in touch with your old friends?

    a) They help you remember past good times and give you a feeling of security for the future.

    b) They remind you of your younger years and make you feel like a kid again.

    c) Old friends are our only true friends.

Answers

Mostly A's: You're knowledgeable about how your physical and emotional health, and expanding your mind power can impact your life now even more strongly than it did in the past. You're taking the time to care for yourself to increase your chances of living the good life.

Mostly B's: Take the time to re-think some of your ideas about your physical and emotional well-being and expanding your mind power. Do some research on the Internet or in the library about health-related topics. Before you know it, you'll be living a healthy lifestyle that will help keep you active for years.

Mostly C's: Give some serious thought to how you're dealing with your health issues, including how you're working to keep your mind engaged. Ask yourself if your approach to health matters is making you feel better or worse. Figure out what you can do to realize the best physical and emotional health, including keeping your mind active. Start your health makeover now.

Chapter 4: Nurture Your Relationships

41. Redefine Family Relationships

*"What greater thing is there for human souls than to feel that
they are joined for life to be with each other in silent unspeakable
memories."—George Eliot (AKA Mary Anne Evans)*

Joy in life at any age springs from relationships with family. Once
you retire, you'll have more time to spend with the people you
love most. You'll also find new challenges, like redefining roles
with your significant other. Here are some questions you'll want
to think about: How much time will you spend together and
apart? What if one of you needs more time to develop your own
interests? How will the other partner adjust to it?

If you still have your parents, how will they fit into your life
now? Because you have more time, will other family members
expect you to be a primary caregiver? What are your feelings
about that? Think about the time you'll devote to children and
grandchildren. What new roles will you play in their lives now
that you're retired? Write about all of these things in your journal, and map out a plan for yourself. Ask yourself how you want
your relationships with your family to stay the same and how you
want them to evolve.

42. Renegotiate Your Primary Relationship

*"I'll walk the dog if you clean the cat litter. On second
thought, I need you to do both. After all, this is my night to
cook."— Conversation between a retired friend and her husband*

When you first retire (especially if you and your mate retire at
the same time), you may experience conflict that rivals what you

went through when you first started living together. As you did then, take the time to adjust to each other's idiosyncracies and personality quirks.

When you retire you have to get to know each other as you did when you first got together. Now the two of you may be completely different people with goals and ambitions you didn't know each other had. It's true that sometimes as we age we go our own separate ways and grow apart but, before we retired, we had more friends and work acquaintances to confide in. Now we have only each other.

You can imagine how many retired women and their mates experience stresses they've never encountered before. Chore wars often abound as do grumblings about someone always being "under foot" and constantly looking over the other's shoulder. That's why it's important to discuss all the changes in your relationship that retirement brings. Talk about what bothers each of you, come to a compromise, and then abide by it.

43. Talk and Listen

"There is no pleasure to me without communication: there is not so much as a sprightly thought comes into my mind that it does not grieve me to have produced alone, and that I have no one to tell it to."—Michel De Montaigne

If you and your mate are smarting from the pinch of relationship problems, it's never too late to see a counselor. First, you may want to try talking with a friend or family member, especially one who has experienced relationship problems after retiring.

It's probably easier if one person retires ahead of the other but, even then, challenges surface because the employed mate sees the partner having more free time and may resent it. If problems surface between you and your mate, you'll both need to talk and listen. Once you address your differences and make a plan to discuss them openly, you've taken the first step to making a compatible, fulfilling relationship.

If you want to improve your communication skills as a couple, many religious organizations, such as Marriage Encounter, offer programs that will help you view one other and your relationship in a positive light. They don't preach and try to convert you; rather, they help you learn how to talk and listen to improve the quality of your relationship.

44. Take Time for Yourselves

Before you think about renewing or intensifying a romantic relationship with your partner, it helps to feel spiritually compatible with each other. If you already have that soul connection, strive to strengthen it. If you don't have it, make an effort to spend meaningful time together to help you appreciate one another more.

Whether you're feeling compatible with your mate or you're working on renewing your relationship, take time out for romantic dinners and walks. Watch a TV show or movie you'll both enjoy.

Find something good about your partner each day and say it. Take the time to express your gratitude for something your partner does for you on a regular basis. Express how you feel by your words and actions to each other. More important, make your body language back up what you say. No matter how angry you are, don't give in to eye-rolling, contemptuous looks, or walking away.

Here are some things you can try to build closeness: Look at your partner when you talk to one another. Don't let yourself be interrupted by cell phones, TV, or computers. Touch each other lovingly and smile more. If you've become strangers, get reacquainted by treating one another with the courtesies you showed each other when you first met. Buy each other small gifts and send short notes, e-mails, or texts to express your appreciation of each other's special qualities.

What was it that first attracted you to one another so that you'd want to be near each other all the time? What would it take to find that feeling again?

45. Rev Up the Romance

"You pierce my soul. I am half agony, half hope...I have loved none but you."—Jane Austen

Assume you've gotten over the hurdle of coexisting with your significant other once you retire. You may have had some conflicts but have put them behind you, thanks to both of your efforts. Maybe, if you're lucky, you didn't have to re-negotiate your relationship.

Now you're thinking it may be fun to put some (or more) romance back into your life. If things have been going well in that department all along, you may want to rev it up a notch. Have you ever noticed that when other aspects of your relationship are running smoothly, romance comes easily?

Once you've renewed your spiritual connection, it's easy to take the next step and grow closer physically. If you have health problems or if you lack energy, you can still keep romance in your life. However, you'll have to work a little harder to find creative ways to enjoy it in ways that you both find pleasing.

Many people, particularly younger people, believe that when people age, they're no longer interested in physical intimacy. The truth is that many older couples find more satisfaction in their romantic lives than some younger people. Physical and psychological closeness become more important to us as we age, and we now have the time to discover ways to enjoy that connection in ways we've never experienced it before.

Kiss, embrace, and cuddle, and the rest will come easily. Do something unpredictable and daring when your mate least expects it. Are you ready to feel the passion?

46. Do You Want to Stay Single or Pair Up?

If you've never had a partner or no longer have one, which quote best applies to your way of thinking?

> *"Marriage has less beauty, but more safety than the single life. It's full of sorrows and full of joys. It lies under more burdens, but it's supported by all the strengths of love, and those burdens are delightful."—16th Century Bishop*

> *"Been single all my life and love it. Why get hitched at this stage of life and ruin all the fun?"—Senior woman overheard in the ladies' room at the Crab Trap Restaurant, Ocean City*

Maybe you're enjoying your freedom if you don't have a partner. If you're single and the prospect of a mate doesn't appeal to you, I won't try to convince you to change your mind. Do what makes you happy. However, maybe finding someone to share your life with is one of your goals. If it is, you may want to start by writing a profile of your perfect match.

Here are some questions for you to ask yourself. What qualities should my ideal partner possess? What type of personality do I favor? Do I like a reserved or a more talkative person? How important is a sense of humor? How important are educational level and shared interests? How much do I value expressions of affection, both physical and verbal? What type of looks do I prefer, or are looks secondary? To what extent does a common religious or ethnic background matter to me? Remember to add a few questions of your own that you consider important to your profile.

Above all, be sure you know the kind of person you're looking for before you begin your search.

47. Let Your Friends Know You're Looking

Once you're decided on the ideal partner, ask your friends if they know any good prospects. If you do ask, be sure they know exactly what type of person you're looking for because their idea of a good partner may not match up with how you envision the perfect mate. Also, you might want to consider singles events sponsored by community or religious organizations. You'll often find them listed in your local newspaper. You may feel more comfortable going this route as the sponsoring agencies often stage these events in a group setting.

You already know that Internet dating services offer another alternative but, if you choose this option, you'll want to proceed with caution. If you decide to date a person you meet online, meet in a public place or have a friend present. Whatever method you choose, there's a good possibility you'll find a partner if you let your friends know that you're actively looking and if you take the initiative to look yourself.

48. Enjoy Your Time with the Kids

"Children begin by loving their parents; after a time they judge them; rarely, if ever, do they forgive them."—Oscar Wilde

If you have grown children, do you see your relationship changing or staying the same? Before you retired, you had limited time to spend with your children. Now that you have the time, do you see yourself having more contact with them? How much do you feel is a fair amount of time to spend with them without intruding on their or your privacy? How do you see the rules changing?

Do you expect them to call you every day, or would you be okay with having them call you at their convenience?

As with everything else, you'll want to strike a balance between having your own life and being an important part of theirs. Discuss guidelines for your new relationship with your children as you go along. Be flexible if things aren't working out the way you'd like, and be open to change. Mainly, enjoy the time you spend with your adult children.

49. Spend Quality Time with Your Grandkids

"A grandmother is a little bit parent, a little bit teacher, and a little bit best friend."—Author Unknown

Grandmom, Mom Mom, Abuela, Granny, Bubbie, Nonna: If you have grandchildren, whatever they call you melts your heart, and you never tire of hearing it. If you were lucky enough to know her, your grandmother was always there to listen without taking sides when you and your parents butted heads or when problems at school or with your friends arose. She listened, didn't judge you, and cared more than anyone else. That's why there's no other relationship like grandmother/grandchild in the universe. Stop for a moment and think of what your grandmother gave you that you'll always remember. I'll bet you can picture her smile, feel her touch, and hear her voice.

If you have grandchildren, you'll want to be an important part of their lives. Think of all the things you remember doing with your grandparents and how you've never forgotten those times and their unconditional love for you. Sure, it's fun to buy your grandkids presents and indulge them, but they'll appreciate and forever remember the little things you do together, whether that is drawing pictures, looking for rare shells on the beach, playing board games, or playing games you invent together.

So go ahead. Dig in the dirt with your grandchild, and don't worry about the bugs and worms. They're the best part.

50. Support Parental Values

When spending time with your grandchildren, keep in mind the importance of supporting their parents' values, disciplinary techniques, and ideas about everything from food to the advice you give them. For example, maybe it bothers you that your children don't carry on the religious traditions you and past generations of family members have worked hard to establish. If you're concerned about this, talk it over with your children, keeping in mind that they'll have the last word with their kids, just as you did with your children.

When we discuss past versus current disciplinary techniques among ourselves and with our children, we can't help but recall how many of us grew up getting a small smack on the hand (or backside) when we talked back or didn't do what our parents said. Now most parents give a time-out or take away toys or privileges. But when you think about it, these may be better consequences after all. Sometimes, parents of our generation and those before us who used physical punishment got caught up in their anger and found it hard to control it. Gentler consequences may be the better way to go, after all.

As for food, it's a standing joke in my family that my kids were allowed to eat sweetened cereal once a year. Most parents today realize that rationing sweets often leads to overindulgence of them. The bottom line is that if your grandkids don't have a lot of restrictions on what they eat, they'll eventually learn that healthy foods taste better than junk foods.

Whether you agree with your grown kids' child-rearing tactics or not, they're the parents, and what they say prevails. If you put everything you do with your grandchildren within this context, it will mean happier times for everyone. That's not to say that, if what the parents are doing seems blatantly out of line to you, you should stand by and say nothing. If you feel you must discuss something that's bothering you, talk to your children about it in a tactful, helpful way. But no hitting: they're way too old for that.

51. Build Memories with Your Parents

"Everybody thinks that as you age, you get old. You don't. Inside I still feel like I'm 18. I just don't look it anymore."— *80-year-old woman to her grown grandson*

Are you fortunate enough to still have one or both parents? If so, now is the time to spend time learning more about them and letting them know how important they are to you. You may want to use old photos as a springboard for them to tell you stories you've never heard before. Even if you've heard them, it doesn't hurt to listen again. They can also write or dictate short anecdotes about their lives based on family photos. If you'd both prefer, you could make a video or record their stories.

Use sentences like this to help them start talking about their experiences: "Think back to when you were growing up"; "Tell me about your grade school friends"; "What was the most fun you had when you were a child?"; "What was high school like for you?"; and "Talk to me about your teachers. Which ones stand out in your memory?" Ask them to tell you what made them happiest and what caused them the most sorrow in their lives. If they could relive one moment, what would it be? What makes them happiest now? What would make them happier still?

52. Say It Now

If you still have your parents, do you feel comfortable talking to them, or do old patterns still persist that prevent you from enjoying one another's company?

Attempt to heal old wounds and to correct whatever things transpired between you and your parents that caused either of you pain. If you had a strained relationship with them in the past, think about how your lives would be better if you could communicate in a way that both of you would find worthwhile. What would it take to get to that point?

If you talk to friends whose parents have died, they'll probably tell you that they'd love to have their parents back if only for a few minutes to tell them something they didn't tell them when they were alive or simply to share a little time with them. If you have anything to say to your parents, say it now. And give them the chance to say what they want to you.

Of course, in a few cases, it's hard to make peace with your parents. I mention this because I have a couple of friends whose parents caused them a lot of pain when they were younger and persist in making their lives miserable as they grow older. If you find yourself in this situation and believe that you can never make peace with your parents, do your best to treat them with respect. However, if the relationship is so toxic that it's irreparable, reach out to other family members and friends as you've probably been doing anyway. They can never take the place of good parents, but they can offer you the love and support that you need.

53. Cherish Your Aging Parents

"Love me when I least deserve it, because that's when I really need it."— Swedish Proverb

When we were younger, we never thought our parents would grow old. As time passed, more than a few of us worried about them getting sick or dying, and it filled us with dread. As we grow older ourselves, it sometimes takes us by surprise to see our parents' appearance and health changing. They may still talk and act like their younger selves, but somehow they seem more vulnerable. And then it dawns on us that we are all they have, that they will begin to depend on us as we have leaned on them throughout the years.

If your parents still enjoy good health, encourage them to keep eating healthy foods, exercising, and staying in touch with friends. What if your parents suffer from serious physical or mental health problems? Sometimes it's a drain on you, particularly if you're their main caregiver, which many women eventually become. Even if you have help, you may feel trapped and alone. And then you may feel guilty because you believe you shouldn't be having negative thoughts about caring for your parents who have sacrificed so much for you.

With all of these conflicting emotions, no wonder you're often drained, confused, and sometimes angry. Allow yourself to express these feelings to a friend, family member, or counselor. Then do something to relieve the pressure you're under.

54. Care for the Caregiver

If you find yourself in the position of caregiver, make the time to get out with friends and by yourself to do the things you love. Don't hesitate to take your family, friends, and neighbors up on their offers to give you a break. You know you'd do the same for them. You'll also want to keep as strong and healthy as you can, both mentally and physically. No matter what problems your parents have, be there for them, and don't forget to tell them how important they are to you and how much you love them.

It's hard to see your parents age in mind and body. It's also frightening because you may start to see it as a harbinger of what's to come. But it may not be that way for you at all. With all the advances in medicine, by the time you're at their stage of life, coping with the challenges of advanced age may become more bearable.

55. Have Fun at Family Gatherings

"Everyone has a couple of weird relatives to contend with, but most people won't admit it. Just laugh along with them or back off. Don't let the goofies get to you."—A friend's mother, age 76

You know what happens sometimes at family gatherings. One of your relatives or a family friend that grates on your nerves shows up. What's the best thing to do? For one thing, don't let the non-stop talker, drinker, criticizer, or complainer ruin the party for you. Enjoy everyone else's company, but keep your physical and psychological distance from the spoiler.

If your crotchety cousin or meddlesome family friend insists on monopolizing you, excuse yourself and move to someone whose company you enjoy. I've resolved at this stage of my life not to spend time with people whose company I don't enjoy. And you can too.

56. Change the Way You Look at Things

"Whenever you're in conflict with someone, there is one factor that can make the difference between damaging your relationship and deepening it. That factor is attitude."—Henry James

You've probably noticed that when people retire they're more easily affected by annoying things that family, friends, and acquaintances sometimes say and do. Because you're not tied up with your job, you have more time to ruminate on simple slights (somebody ignoring or not including you) or larger indignities (somebody saying nasty things to or about you).

Tell yourself that, before you react, you'll try to change the way you look at the situation. Imagine that you're embroiled in a disagreement with a family member. Nobody's willing to budge. Give the issue that's upsetting you another look from a different angle. You may get some insights that will help ease the conflict. Once you view a situation, whether a standoff or a conflict, in a different way, the answer about how to handle it will often come to you when you decide to change the way you perceive it.

57. Surround Yourself with Positive People

If you find yourself in a conflict with someone, be it a friend or family member, step back for a while to give both of you some needed space. If that doesn't work, ask what would make the other person feel better about the situation. See what he or she comes up with, and go from there. If you can compromise, try that.

If the person in question refuses to compromise, at least you'll know where you stand. Sometimes simply backing away from a person who grates on your nerves will do the trick. Don't give the person positive or negative attention. It's best not to respond if someone persistently engages you in an argument.

On the other hand, if a person insults or berates you, respond as you would to a bully. We're used to thinking of kids as bullies but, as you probably know, bullying abounds among all age groups, especially in the workplace, in social settings, and in senior developments and communities. If the trouble persists or things get worse, try using a firm but brief comeback (backed up with strong body language), such as "Don't say that," or "I need you to stop now." Avoid this person at all costs.

The main thing is to surround yourself with people who give you a positive rather than a negative feeling whenever you're around them. Why settle for less?

Chapter 4: Takeaways

- Expect a readjustment in your relationship with your mate when one or both of you retires.

- Work with your partner to build new and better ways of relating to one another.

- Build closeness with your partner by choosing activities you both enjoy.

- Enhance your physical relationship. Be creative.

- Strike a happy balance between having your own life and enjoying a rewarding relationship with your grown children.

- Abide by your children's guidelines for raising your grandkids.

- Make peace with your parents while you still have time.

- View conflicts with family members in a different way to find a solution.

- Accept only the best interactions and treatment from family and friends.

Quiz #3: Nurture Your Relationships

What kinds of things will you do to nurture your relationships with family and friends? Take the quiz and see if you're on the right track.

1. What can help you enjoy your family's company during retirement?

    a) Keep in constant contact with them. That will show them you care.

    b) To avoid conflicts, always say *yes*. As people age, it's not worth it to argue.

    c) Spend time thinking about how you want your familial relationships to stay the same and how you want them to evolve.

2. After you retire, it's helpful if you and your partner

    a) spend as much time as you can together.

    b) leave each other alone. Too much togetherness can hurt a relationship.

    c) talk and listen to each other, and address your differences.

3. To help rev up your romantic life

    a) strew rose petals near your bed and rustle up a silky negligee.

    b) be brutally honest about what you don't like about your partner.

    c) make time to do the things you both enjoy.

4. If you're single and looking for love, you may want to start by

    a) going online and checking out dating sites.
    b) letting your friend set you up on a blind date.
    c) writing a profile of your perfect match.

5. What is one of the most important factors in having a good relationship with your adult children?

    a) Letting them live their own lives—they don't need you to tell them what to do.
    b) Calling them a few times a day to ask what's new.
    c) Striking a balance between having your own life and being an important part of theirs.

6. When spending time with grandchildren, it helps to

    a) tell them something once and expect them to do it.
    b) spoil them every chance you get. After all, what are grandparents for?
    c) support their parents' child-raising values.

7. If you're fortunate enough to have one or both parents, now is the time to

    a) ask them for their best advice about dealing with any problems you have.
    b) keep hounding them to put their affairs in order.
    c) learn more about them and let them know how important they are to you.

8. If you're a caregiver or think you may become one,

    a) try not to think about your feelings of anger and resentment.
    b) allow yourself to sink into self-pity once in a while.

   c) ask for help from family and friends, and stay mentally
      and physically strong.

9. What can you do if a person who constantly annoys you shows
up at a family gathering?

   a) Try to pacify the bothersome guest. Take the time to
      be extra kind.
   b) Tell the person in no uncertain terms to back off.
   c) Keep your physical and psychological distance from the
      person.

10) Before you react to a family member or a friend who
constantly upsets you,

   a) think about kissing and making up. Life is short.
   b) consider what you did to cause the person to act that
   way.
   c) try to change the way you look at the situation and
   then seek a solution.

Answers

Mostly A's: With a little more effort, you'll be on the right path.
Think of your close relationships with family and friends, and ask
yourself how best to address the issues that come up from time
to time. Be open and honest with them, and ask them to respond
in kind.

Mostly B's: Re-think how you deal with family and friends,
especially at this time of life when you're spending more time
with them. Avoid being too blunt, but don't try to solve problems by smoothing them over. If your relationships often cause

you problems, ask yourself how you can be proactive in finding solutions.

Mostly C's: You're satisfied with how you're getting along with your family and friends. You're willing to compromise and look creatively at each situation that comes up. You seek harmony in your relationships, but not at the expense of your mental health. You're doing your best to nurture your positive relationships and to deal with those that aren't working.

Chapter 5: Relish Every Minute

58. Enjoy a Mini Vacation

By now you're starting to think seriously about experiencing the most joy you've had at any time of your life. Although we know we're only on this earth for a while, we tend to put off the things we most want to do. We tell ourselves that we'll get around to doing all these things one of these days. But for most people, that day never comes, especially for us women. Our responsibilities often take priority, and we sometimes feel guilty if we do something we'd perceive as wild or frivolous. Now it's time to shed those beliefs. Are you ready?

Of course, we all have things to do like paying bills and keeping our households running, hopefully with our partner's cooperation, if we have one. But this is your time, like no other time before, to do the things you've never had time to do when you were going to school, working, or raising kids.

One thing you can do to help you start loving every minute is to take a mini vacation. It won't take much time and will do wonders for your happiness quotient. You can spend as much or as little money as you decide. Use your creative mind to visualize something you'd love to do to get away from it all, and make the plans to do it. Don't think of all the reasons it wouldn't work; just decide to do it, and take all the necessary steps. Once you start, it will be easy.

Here are some ideas you can do right from home. Gather some videos you've been wanting to see, and plan to watch them over a few days. Is there a book on your list that you've looked forward to reading? Order it now or find it in the library. Allow yourself the luxury of spending a couple of hours a day watching the films or reading the book. Turn off your cell phone. Make yourself comfortable, and immerse yourself in things you truly enjoy. Order in, eat out, or cook something you don't usually make if you enjoy cooking and don't think of it as a chore.

If you have a significant other, watch the movie together or read the same book; appreciate and discuss it as a couple. Would you rather take your mini vacation alone? That's okay, too. Your mate will find something to enjoy solo, and then you can share your experiences later.

Would you rather leave home to take your mini vacation? You don't have to go far or plan extensively to make your vacation a success. Plan a one or two-night trip to the city if you live in the country, and to a more bucolic place if you live in the hustling, bustling city. If you opt for the city, book a concert or a show you'd love to see, and reserve a hotel that's close to everything: sidewalk cafés, museums, and shops. If you choose the country, explore a small town you love or one you'd love to visit. Stay in an out-of-the-beaten-path bed and breakfast or a cozy country inn.

Your mini vacation is what you choose to make it. Write out a few possibilities in your journal, choose the one you'd like best, and block out time to make it happen. If your mini-vacation made you feel relaxed and happy, why not plan another one?

59. Renew Your Life with Travel

"The world is a book, and those who do not travel read only a page."—St. Augustine

Whether you've traveled all your life or you've never had time to travel, consider planning a trip to your dream destination. As we get older, many of us want to go places near and far but find ourselves put off by the hassles of arranging the trip, waiting around in airports, and taking the long journey. But once we get there, everything usually falls into place, and we wonder why we didn't take more trips in our lifetime. We find ourselves able to communicate with people we meet even though we hardly speak their language. We become more adventurous and try foods we may never have dared taste before. We also find our way around with the generous help of citizens and tourists alike.

Do you enjoy traveling by yourself? You can do what you want when you feel like it without worrying about a travel partner's preferences. If you don't have a partner or your partner doesn't want to travel, don't let that stop you. You'll be surprised at how easy it is to recruit a family member or friend as a traveling partner. If no one can go with you, singles cruises abound, and many organizations sponsor trips where you can travel with likeminded people and forge new friendships. Additionally, many seniors love to make memories by going on trips with their children and grandchildren.

How much of your own country have you seen? Are there places you've heard others speak highly of that you still haven't visited? Arrange a motor trip, or travel by train or plane, whichever you prefer, and plan to see some sights you haven't seen in your own country.

If planning the trip yourself seems mind-boggling, visit a travel agent or ask a friend who has been there for suggestions about where to go and what to see. Post a message on social media sites asking for recommendations; people will be more than willing to offer helpful ideas about how you can fully appreciate your chosen destination.

Another route you may want to take is arranging a house exchange with someone in this country or abroad. It would cut costs and give you more of a feeling for the people because you'd be living among them and become a part of them for the time you visited. You can easily find these agencies on the Internet, and senior organizations, such as AARP, also offer listings for house exchanges in their publications.

Whatever trip you decide to take, be sure to keep a brief record of the places you visited and your reactions to them. You probably won't want to spend a lot of time writing in your journal, but you'll want to remember everything you experienced so you can talk about it later and relive it when you do.

Write twitter-sized entries in your journal or a small notebook you can keep in your purse to record travel impressions. Record memorable experiences, funny episodes, and mishaps. They're all worth remembering and re-telling. And don't forget to take pictures with people in all of them, both the people who accompany you and new friends you make, rather than photographing only the stunningly beautiful scenes you'll see. It's the people that make the trip. Don't you think?

60. Lose Your Sense of Time

When I find a book I like (I happen to like suspense novels), I feel like I'm right there in the character's head: heart pumping, bolting from my pursuer, racing to safety, hoping I'll make it out alive. Suddenly, I look at the clock and it's a couple of hours later. Where the heck was I all that time? —66-year-old-retired realtor I met in a bookstore

Did you ever notice that when you're truly engaged in a task, enjoying one of your hobbies or interests alone or with friends, you lose track of time? You look at the clock, and the next thing you know, it's three hours later. But that's a good feeling because you know you spent that block of time doing something you love. You didn't waste time because you lost yourself in something meaningful to you, enjoying a hobby like scrapbooking, reading, writing, gardening, or playing a card game with friends.

What kinds of things do you participate in that give you this feeling of bliss, this sensation of time not moving? Can you think of even more activities to try so that you can experience that sense of oneness with what you're doing?

You probably find that feeling of timelessness lacking when you're doing things that don't excite you, such as cleaning or organizing your finances. And yet, sometimes you can actually lose yourself in these everyday chores if you allow yourself. You may want to help yourself capture that same feeling you get when you're doing something you love by considering how you'll feel when you see the finished product as you're going about your job, whether it's balancing your checkbook or clearing away clutter. If so, take it one step at a time, and throw yourself into the job until you complete it. If you try not to focus on the drudgery aspect of a chore and don't focus on how much time it takes, it can actually become a gratifying experience.

Naturally, we're more apt to lose our sense of time when we're doing something that appeals to us. You'll want to think of some ways to add more of these hobbies and activities to your life so that you experience more of this timeless bliss. You may want to keep a brief record in your journal of your experiences with losing yourself in a task.

List activities that gave you that sensation and how you felt when you performed them. You don't have to use complete sentences; instead, use a few adjectives to describe your experience. Dream up one or two other things that may create similar feelings for you, and promise yourself to make it a point to try them.

Whatever gives you this sense of total engagement in what you're doing, this sense that time is not of the essence and that it's suspended, if only for a while, helps add meaning and purpose to your life. Give yourself opportunities to experience more of these events that make you forget about the clock, and you will discover a more pleasurable existence.

61. Find Solo Hobbies to Enjoy

"When a habit begins to cost money, it's called a hobby."—Jewish Proverb

With all the gizmos and gadgets our grandkids possess, they still sometimes complain about boredom. However, we as women growing older rarely consider boredom a problem; in fact, many of us have never experienced it. Maybe that's because when we grew up if we said we were bored, our mothers would counter with, "Bored? There's no such thing. I'll get you out of that state in no time. You can start by helping me." We'd take our cue, scoot out of the room and pretend to start on our homework so that our moms wouldn't chase after us with a vacuum cleaner or a toilet bowl brush.

It's understandable, however, that once in a while, boredom can strike anyone, especially retired women. One reason may be because we have so many options now that we don't know where to begin. If you ever get in a rut and believe that finding a new hobby would help, brainstorm some ideas with yourself or a friend. Use your journal to generate ideas.

List some hobbies you've wanted to try. As you did when you brainstormed before, begin to write without letting your logical brain intrude. Let the ideas flow freely, and don't think of how outlandish they seem or what you'll have to do to get started. Once you've filled a page with your list, circle the ones that excite you. Narrow that list down to two or three, and you're on your way.

Here are some ideas to get you started: Think about a craft you'd like to try, such as knitting, rug hooking, photography, greeting card making, or scrapbooking. You can also find more novel ideas for different kinds of crafts on the Internet, like decoupage and wreath making. Sign up for a class and see if you like it enough to invest in it with your time and money. If you already collect recipes and love cooking, find a cooking class in your area or sign up for an online class. After looking into it to see if it's right for you, sign up and start creating dishes your family and friends will rave about.

Did you ever think of blogging as a hobby? Think about what you do best, be it writing, giving advice, parenting, cooking, or any other topic you excel in. If you're not sure of what to focus on, think of an area in which people often seek your advice and start with that. Many blog sponsors are user-friendly and will walk you through every step. You'll also find books galore on the topic. In no time, you'll become an expert blogger. You'll also gain a new network of friends.

Once you get started with your new hobby, you'll beat the boredom blues. You may be tempted to use your mother's words: "Bored? There's no such thing."

62. Enjoy Hobbies You Love with Friends and Family

If you're searching for a hobby you can enjoy with family or friends, you won't have to look very far. You may already participate in a book club. Instead of discussing the books (in addition to the eating and chatting many of us do), try adding a twist to your book club format.

For example, members can agree ahead of time to consider different components of the book and take responsibility for one area of discussion such as plot, theme, dialogue, language usage, memorable passages, narration, characters, or setting. Another thing you can do is have participants assume the personalities of major and minor characters in the novel by using their characters' distinctive language and mannerisms. Members take turns interviewing or talking informally to the characters to uncover motivation, plot twists and turns, theme, and story outcome. If you're discussing a non-fiction book, you can stage a panel discussion or debate about the pros and cons of the author's ideas. Recruit a moderator and let the controversy begin.

Do you enjoy playing board games? Arrange to have a game night with your friends on a regular basis, gifting winners with small prizes. Guests bring appetizers or desserts. Rotate the games you play, so that everyone has a chance to enjoy a favorite game. If you prefer computer games, you'll find many you can play with friends on the Web. You can even play against your competition in different locations.

Have you always wanted to learn a different language but never got around to it? Buy a language program or borrow one from the library, and learn with a family member or friend. You and your conversation partner will want to practice on a regular basis, eventually building up to themed conversations (for example, greetings, weather, family, politics, or thoughts about what's going on in your lives, your community, or in the world). Be sure to buy a pocket dictionary or an app for your mobile digital device to help build vocabulary. You can also find excellent podcasts showcasing native speakers offering language instruction on the Internet.

If you're learning Spanish, watch the news on the Spanish channel to help you speak more formally. If you want to polish your informal conversational skills, watch soap operas or talk shows. You'll find many Spanish channels on cable. Some other nationalities also offer their own programs.

Do you remember when you were growing up and someone in your house set up a card table with a jigsaw puzzle? Every time family members walked by the table, they added a few more pieces to help the puzzle progress. By the end of the week, the table featured a completed puzzle. Sometimes the puzzle contained a thousand pieces, but somehow it always ended up as a beautiful picture—until someone messed it up, threw the pieces in the box, and brought out another. Try setting up a puzzle in your family room and see what happens when company comes. Don't be surprised if your grandchildren beat you in creating the picture-perfect puzzle.

When looking for a hobby for two or more people, think about how you can make it creative and fun for all involved. The possibilities are limitless.

63. Sample New Experiences

"A mind that is stretched by a new experience can never go back to its old dimensions."—Oliver Wendell Holmes

As we grow older, we sometimes shy away from new experiences. What holds us back? Sometimes it's fear: physical (as in "I'm terrified of heights, so I don't want to Parasail"), or psychological (as in "I'd like to de-clutter my house, but I'm afraid of losing some of my prized possessions and my history").

Amy, a friend of mine from the east coast, has always wanted to visit the west coast, but her nerves get the better of her when she thinks about flying. Last spring she decided it was time to make that trip. An invitation from a college friend she hadn't seen in years provided a strong incentive. She took the first step and talked to a counselor friend who helped her overcome her fear of air travel. Amy says that thoughts of flying still give her butterflies in her stomach (although their flutters now feel more like a gentle breeze), but she's glad she took her dream trip.

Next year she and her sister plan to tour France, where they're looking forward to attending a cooking school and exploring the French countryside. They're already starting to prepare for their adventure by listening to language tapes and podcasts. Her only regret? That she didn't start traveling sooner.

Other fears, like fear of failure, can keep us from trying new experiences. A local café features an open mic where people read and recite their poetry. You've always loved poetry and would like to try your hand at writing and reciting it. Then the fears start creeping in: What if nobody likes what I wrote? What if everyone starts talking or looks bored when I'm reading? What if I bomb?

Why not change the way you think about trying a new experience? Try it once and see how it goes. If you don't like the way you feel after you try it, you can always return to your old way of thinking, but I'll bet you never will. Banish the negative thoughts (most of them never materialize anyway), and experience the joy of creating something of your very own and sharing it with others. The important thing is that you lose yourself in the experience and grow from it, not that you become a famous poet or whatever else you're aiming to do.

Another thing you can do to sample new experiences is to try new foods. Go out to an ethnic restaurant instead of your favorite seafood stop or hamburger haven. Try sushi or tofu if you're used to eating a tuna sandwich or salad for lunch. Ask friends for suggestions, and savor new foods you've never eaten. If you're used to bland, try spicy; if you yearn for sweet, try sour, or mix the two. You may find that you can learn to appreciate foods you've shied away from all your life.

Think about the movies you watch on TV and in the theater. If you're used to watching modern movies, give old movies a second look. Watch one with your partner or a friend and talk about how they differ from newer ones in plot, message, and delivery. Do you favor more subtlety in romantic scenes or do you prefer raw reality? How does the sentimentality factor compare in the older and newer films? Do you find the vintage ones more touching and heartfelt than the more recent ones, or do you think they're overdone and unrealistic?

Watching and discussing different types of movies from the ones you're used to can make you think and spark fascinating conversations and debates. Consider some new experiences you'd like to sample, and promise yourself you'll try one soon.

64. Immerse Yourself in Creative Outlets

"The deepest experience of the creator is feminine, for it is the experience of receiving and bearing."—Ranier Maria Rilke

We as women have always been creators: creators of new ideas, movers and shakers, motivators, and bearers of life. It's only natural that our creative muses will move us to take part in those artistic adventures that lift our lives out of the ordinary and transform them into the extraordinary.

Think about what you love doing in your spare time. It's often something you've felt a fondness for since childhood, such as art, writing, or crafts. Your creative mind can be a voice that whispers to you in your quiet moments and says, "I'm here waiting for you. Are you ready? Please listen and answer. I'll help you."

Maybe you haven't spent much time indulging your creative impulses over the years due to feelings of guilt over spending time on yourself or the need to complete mundane tasks that can usually wait until tomorrow. Think about what kinds of creative adventures you'd find stimulating, ones that would excite you enough to keep you fully engrossed and engaged.

Have you ever thought about taking up drawing or painting? Maybe you'd prefer photography. As with any creative medium, think about doing it for the sheer joy of it; when you first start out, don't think about selling your work unless you want to. That may come in time. For now, find satisfaction in creating something you and those dear to you will love to look at and appreciate.

Draw, paint, or photograph subjects that mean something to you personally. You may want to think about focusing on a theme: family, friends, nature, pets, or people of different age groups, such as babies, teenagers, or the elderly. Ask what your artwork is telling you about these people, nature, or pets.

Even though they are similar, how are they different? What do the faces and body language of the people and animals tell you? What is inside them that you bring out in your artistic interpretation? Ponder nature as the poet, painter, and mystic William Blake did in his poem "The Tiger" as you paint or photograph it. Do you think its symmetry is random, or is there some divine scheme behind it all? Let your creativity help you ponder the deeper questions and bring you to a greater understanding of your life and the universe in which you live.

Have you ever thought about writing? Perhaps you've been recording your own thoughts in a journal as you've thought about the topics in this book, giving them your own unique perspective on the subjects, and producing a tangible record of how you will change your life for the better.

If you enjoy writing, what type of writing most moves you: fiction, non-fiction, or poetry? Maybe you're thinking about publishing something you wrote. As with art, concentrate on the pleasure of writing rather than getting published. You will know if and when you're ready to send your work out to the world. If you decide to publish, start putting your ideas out on social media or begin writing a blog on your favorite subject.

Maybe you show your best creativity by creating masterpieces with your hands by knitting, quilting, crocheting, or doing other handicrafts. As with art and writing, you may want to create products for your own pleasure and that of your relatives and friends, or you may eventually decide to sell them at craft fairs.

Whatever artistic channels you decide to use to enhance your life quality, think about how using your creative powers helps you view the bigger picture of why we're here and what we're about. Most of all, think about how what we create brings us a little closer to the divine and the eternal in each of us.

65. Showcase Your Talents

"I thought writing would be a wonderful second career, but I just got my 42nd rejection slip for a novel that took me three years to write. Should I keep submitting, think about self-publishing, or keep writing for the sheer joy of it and let whatever happens happen?"— Question from Lilly, age 64, retired teacher and aspiring writer, to a fiction workshop leader at a local writers' conference

Have you thought seriously about sharing your creations with the world by publishing, exhibiting, or selling your work? Why not try going public with your work and seeing what happens. Once you do, it helps to take a neutral stance. Don't hope too strongly, but don't go into it believing it will never happen. If you publish, sell your paintings or build a booming craft business, you'll rejoice, but if you don't, you'll still be okay. You won't be too disappointed if it doesn't work out if you go into it with a realistic attitude.

However, if you're attempting to go public with your talents and you've developed your talent in the best way possible, I believe you should never give up. Modify your expectations, change things around so that you succeed the best you can, but never say *I can't do this* or *I give up*.

If you're trying to progress to the next level and pitch your talents to a wider audience, learn everything you can about how to deliver your work to the public. Read online message boards and blogs about your chosen field. Find a mentor, someone who can guide you thorough the process. If you're a writer, attend a writer's conference and make connections with other writers; if you're an artist, view exhibits and network with other artists; if you create crafts, talk to other crafters to learn more about the business end of selling your work.

It's vital if you're selling a product to learn all you can about marketing and sales techniques. For example, if you're hosting a house party to sell your jewelry or other handiwork, be sure that you make prices clearly visible and that you spend more time promoting your products than chatting and thinking about the guacamole and punch.

If you're a writer trying to sell your writing and things don't seem to be moving, try a different approach. You may want to look into self-publishing or using an e-book company. Of course, you'll need to proceed with caution as some companies may be more interested in taking your money than in helping you. If you decide to self-publish or use an e-book company that will prepare your files for a cost, be prepared to publicize your work, as these companies, unlike traditional publishers, leave that part of the business to you. But be advised: today many traditional publishers expect you to promote your books on social media and arrange your own speaking tours.

Similarly, if you're an artist in any medium, you'll need to work hard to promote your products. If you decide to sell your art or crafts over the Internet, you may want to hire a professional to create an attractive website and present your items in the most appealing light possible to draw traffic to your site. If you're using an established website for buyers and sellers, you'll also need to make your products stand out from all the rest.

The bottom line is that while it's fun to showcase your talents and make a name for yourself, you'll need to be prepared to put up with rejection and to work harder than you've worked in your entire life. If you believe that the glory is not worth the effort you have to put into it, maybe you'd feel more content sharing your talents with your family circle and friends. It's up to you. Whatever route you decide to take, you can make it equally pleasurable.

66. Sharpen Skills You Already Have

Another thing you can do to help you enjoy your life more fully is to sharpen skills you already have so that you can use them for your own pleasure or in the workplace for fun and profit.

Have you always dreamed of earning an undergraduate or advanced degree in a subject you love? Don't hesitate because of your age or fear of competing with younger students. Many women returning to college experience a sense of exhilaration and renewal when they start a degree program and find themselves warmly accepted by students their children's or even their grandchildren's ages. These younger students value their older peers' advice and experience, while the returning students get to see their chosen course of study and life from a fresh perspective, a win-win situation for both parties.

Look into your local community college or university. Find an expert in the counseling division to help you map out your program, and if you're interested in earning an undergraduate degree, be sure to ask about the credit for life experience program, which may shorten your expenditures of time and money. Also, investigate online courses given by reputable schools if you'd prefer distance learning to studying at a campus.

Maybe you've reached your educational aspirations and have already earned the degrees you needed in your chosen field. If you're interested in improving your skills in the hobby or creative pursuit you love above all others, you won't have to look far to find a way to reach your goal.

If you love playing a musical instrument, sign up for individual or group lessons. It's a hobby you can easily lose yourself in and spend many happy hours playing your favorite songs and improvising. Revive interest in an instrument you played before, or learn to play one you've never played before.

Find a teacher who will encourage you to learn at your own pace and provide you with the type of instruction that resonates best with you. Do you love classical, or do you prefer jazz? Do you want to learn by studying sheet music or by learning chords you can use to help you write your own music so that you can improvise? Look for a music teacher who will work with you to give you exactly what you want to know and will consider your unique learning style.

Have you always loved dancing but never had time to learn it? Make a date with your partner to take dancing lessons. Group lessons make it easy to learn and eliminate some of the pressure of being constantly on stage and in the limelight while you're learning.

If you'd prefer to hone your dancing skills without taking lessons, look in a search engine for the type of dancing that interests you (for example: dances from the fifties and sixties, disco, line or country dancing, or contemporary). Find places that offer instruction in your area, and make it a point to go there with a partner or friend. If you don't enjoy the ambience or the crowd, try another location. But keep on dancing. If you have no one to go with, go alone and find new friends.

No matter which skill you're aiming to enhance, it's vital, especially at this stage of your life, to find the right teacher. This instructor will be one who facilitates and guides your learning, letting you take the lead, rather than telling you what to do. Your ideal teacher will take into consideration how you learn best and will consider and apply your own personal learning style while teaching you, be it visual (seeing), auditory (hearing), or kinesthetic (hands on).

Sharpening skills you already have is a great way to fire up your life. You already know the basics and have the aptitude and the desire to learn more. All you have to do is find a way to do it, and then let the fun begin.

67. Learn New Skills

If you've always wanted to delve into a subject but put your interests on hold because you needed to study something more practical that would land you a lucrative job, think about learning that new subject now.

Some retired women have started new careers in areas completely unrelated to the fields they worked in their entire lives and have experienced great success. In some cases, they have entered careers that didn't require new training. They simply employed skills they already had such as speaking ability, dealing with people, trouble-shooting, problem solving, rapport building, teamwork, and computing skills.

In Chapter One, you met Dr. Beth, a retired physician who currently works in retail. She didn't take any courses in sales, but because she has had years of experience interacting with patients in her medical practice, she knows how to communicate effectively with people. As with her medical practice, she keeps her customers in the shoe department coming back because they know she genuinely cares about them and will always treat them ethically.

On the other hand, some women seeking second careers find that taking courses helped them find jobs completely unrelated to their original fields of study. Elisa, a trial attorney nearing retirement, decided to use her people skills and persuasive abilities to start her own business. She took a few courses in computers at the local community college and used that knowledge base to launch a highly successful computer repair business. Now she travels around the country offering her expertise to large and mid-size companies.

If you're contemplating learning new job skills so that you can start a second career, figure out what you want to do based on your interests and aptitudes. Ask yourself if you prefer working closely with people or if you'd rather work by yourself. Think about whether you like working with details or if you'd rather focus on broader issues. Do numbers excite you, or do you find them boring? Are you a self-starter, or do you prefer more structure?

After pondering these questions, ask yourself what types of jobs you can find that complement your interests and skills. How much if any training would your new vocation require? Think about whether you'd like to use your new skills in a full or part-time job. Maybe you'll want to learn new skills for your own enjoyment rather than as a route to future employment.

If you decide to reenter the work force, find out what types of training programs can best help prepare you for the job. Talk to people you know who work in the job that interests you. Ask them about the pleasures and pitfalls of the job. Have them give you their best advice about finding success and satisfaction in this job. Peruse search engines for articles and blogs to find out more first-hand information about jobs you think will match your new skills.

Research employment opportunities near where you live to determine job availability in your chosen field. Once you've established that there is a need for your new skills, you can start investigating training programs in your area. Compare courses of study in local colleges to help you learn these new skills: what types of courses you need and how many, how long it takes to complete the program, and overall cost. Shop around to find the best program for your needs. Look for online evaluations of programs you're researching.

What new skill have you always wanted to try? Think about using it in a part or full time job, or simply for your own intellectual and spiritual growth. It's never too late to learn a new skill.

68. Doing Nothing is Okay—Sometimes

Throughout this book, we've talked about different ways to reinvent and revitalize your life. Did you ever think that doing nothing might be one of them? That's right—just sitting there and watching the world go by, no pressure, no striving, or worrying about accomplishing something.

I'm not talking about meditation that brings you to a state of nirvana and helps you leave your tensions and worries behind. Doing nothing means sitting there with no goal in mind, thinking about nothing in particular: reading, basking in the sun, or simply daydreaming with no concern for anything but relaxing and giving yourself totally to that sensation. It's not even living in the moment because you're not really aware of the moment. You're not thinking of anything you have to do or where you have to be. You just are, and you're loving it.

Some women tell me that it's impossible for them to do nothing. That old bugaboo guilt always gets in their way. The voice inside you may say, "How can you waste time like that? Are you an old lady in a rocking chair waiting to die? Get up off your duff and do something."

If that's what you're thinking, think again. It's okay to do nothing sometimes. It will actually help you become more productive when you need to be. It will restore your energy and sense of purpose because it takes you away, if only for a short time, from all the to-dos that dominate your life. Doing nothing can give you the sense of freedom and abandon you felt as a child when you played outside in the sunshine, not hearing when your mom called you in for dinner, or the feeling you got when you pretended your stuffed animals were real and you let them talk to each other with your voice.

When you're doing nothing, you can be doing other things but you don't have to do anything at all. If you want to do something while you're doing nothing, consider these ideas: Swing on a glider on a porch in the sunshine and let your mind wander; watch a favorite comedy show on TV and give in to your impulse to release loud belly laughs; or set out for a ride in the country with no particular destination in mind. Stroll around the park, swing high on the swings, and eat a picnic lunch of your favorite foods.

Consider this for a journal entry: write a poem or short piece about what you learned from doing nothing. How did the experience make you feel? Describe it using comparisons and vivid adjectives. What is your favorite way to do nothing, the one that helps you completely relax and come out of it feeling rejuvenated?

You get the idea. Doing nothing is actually doing something. If you do nothing every so often, it will rejuvenate you and motivate you to become more creative and productive. It's okay to do nothing—sometimes.

69. Add Music to the Mix

"If you are sad, remember a beautiful song you know. It is really something living. It can bring you to the place where it was created out of light, and you can feel that for a moment."—Hafiz

Dick Clark, the legendary host of American Bandstand, once said, "Music is the soundtrack of your life." I'm sure you've had the experience of hearing certain songs and having them transport you to another time and place. The song brings back the sights and sounds of dancing on a moonlit pavilion with your high school beau; working at your first waitress job with the jukebox blaring the Big Bopper; attending a special celebration like a birthday where you heard "Happy, Happy Birthday, Baby"; or a graduation party where they played "Graduation Day."

When you hear the song, you feel like you're there again. The joys, sorrows, and all the powerful emotions you felt when you heard the song back then take over, and you experience them again. We know that the past is gone and that we can never go back, but we can recapture the sensations we felt when we were there, both the happy and sad times. Hearing the musical soundtrack of our lives helps us look back at who we were and celebrate the women we've become. We can see how far we've progressed when we think of where we once were. Listening to music is the vehicle that can take us there.

Music can also offer you a delightful accompaniment to the soundtrack of your present life. Listen to your favorite music any way you choose: play records (many online stores offer turntables to play your 45s and 78s) or listen to CDs or your favorite radio station. Start or expand your collection of favorite songs by downloading them to your mobile digital device. If you're not sure how, ask your kids, grandkids, or someone at your electronics store to help.

Learn about a new type of music you've never paid much attention to before. If you're into Oldies, interject some jazz into the mix. If you like disco, give blues a chance. If you prefer contemporary, see how the big band era moves you. Expand your musical repertoire and add more listening pleasure to your life.

Playing music helps boost your mood and comforts you when you're feeling low. Music has magical powers in that it can help you rebound and set you back on your feet again. It also motivates you when you have to do something you don't feel like doing like humdrum household tasks or running errands. If you're stressed, the right kind of music will calm you down. Spark your creativity by playing music that inspires you. Nothing makes exercise more bearable than music, and the livelier, the better.

For everything you want to do there's music to fit your fancy. Music is as individual as you are. Some women find classical music inspiring when they want to activate their creative powers while others prefer jazz. Try playing music from the 50s, 60s, and 70s (particularly disco) when you're doing routine chores. The fast-paced songs can make you move more quickly and get the job done faster.

When you're feeling sad or upset, music can help comfort you. Sometimes it helps to let the tears out: the words and music of your favorite song can make you feel better and give you a new perspective on a problem.

Play music often. Dance, sing, and let yourself go. Play it when you're alone and when you're among friends. It's the soundtrack of your life that bridges the past to the present and will endure deep into the future.

Chapter 5: Takeaways

- Plan a mini vacation to enjoy at home or away.

- Renew your life by traveling near or far.

- Search for hobbies and activities that help you lose your sense of time.

- Beat boredom by finding a new hobby.

- Find unique ways to enjoy hobbies with friends and family.

- Welcome new experiences, and don't let fears hold you back.

- Find a creative outlet that will lift your life out of the ordinary.

- Showcase your talents by going public with your artistic interests.

- Build on skills you already have to expand your possibilities.

- Learn a new skill to help you start a second career.

- Do nothing sometimes to rejuvenate yourself.

- Play music often to enhance your life experiences.

Quiz #4: Relish Every Minute

What simple things can you do to help you gain more satisfaction from each day? Take this quiz to see how much effort you're putting into making your life more fulfilling.

1. Which kind of mini vacation will provide you with the most satisfaction?

    a) One that will boost your happiness quotient

    b) One that takes you as far away as possible

    c) One you spend by yourself

2. You'll gain more pleasure from travel if you

    a) keep a record of places you visited and your reactions to them.

    b) avoid being friendly to people you meet on your trip.

    c) Rule out any kind of travel that makes you nervous.

3. We're more likely to lose our sense of time when

    a) we're completely engaged in a task.

    b) we try to complete our tasks quickly to get them over with.

    c) we forget about watching the clock.

4. If you suffer from bouts of boredom,

    a) find some interesting hobbies you can enjoy alone.

    b) there's plenty of work you can do around the house, so get busy.

    c) tell yourself that everyone feels bored sometimes. It will pass.

5. How can you enhance your enjoyment of hobbies you share with your friends and family?

    a) Add a creative twist to how you participate in them.

    b) Keep taking part in your hobbies in the same old way. There's comfort in predictability.

    c) Enjoy your hobbies on a more regular basis.

6. What is one way that using your creative powers can help you?

    a) They'll help you view the bigger picture of why we're here and what we're about.

    b) They'll help you get rich quickly.

    c) They'll help you gain more admirers.

7. If you're having trouble succeeding when attempting to showcase your talents, you may want to

    a) modify your expectations but never give up.

    b) move on to something else and stop being a sore loser.

    c) give up your idea of going public. The pain of rejection isn't worth it.

8. When you're sharpening skills you already have, it's vital to

    a) find a teacher who respects your learning style.

    b) find a teacher who tells you exactly what to do.

    c) find the teacher who has the best personality.

9. If you're aiming to learn new job skills, you'll need to consider

    a) your interests and aptitudes.

    b) whether you're too old to enter your chosen field.

    c) your family's and friends' opinions.

10. Doing nothing is okay sometimes because it

   a) restores your energy and sense of purpose.
   b) reminds you that working too hard ruins your health.
   c) encourages you to get more rest as you get older.

11. Listening to the musical soundtrack of your life helps you

   a) look back at who you were and celebrate who you've become.
   b) realize how much more fun you had when you were younger.
   c) acknowledge that the songs of the past were better than any music before or since.

Answers

Mostly A's: You have a good understanding about how to use each moment to enhance your satisfaction by using your free time wisely. You know how to live your life with gusto by yourself and with others.

Mostly B's: Concentrate on making your down time more meaningful. Give yourself a needed break from chores and your to-do list even if it means doing nothing once in a while. Don't let your fears prevent you from exploring new possibilities to make your life more adventurous.

Mostly C's: Think about some innovative ways to help bring more enjoyment to your life. Think out of the box to help you make the best of the talents you possess. Thinking positively about your aptitudes and abilities will add a new dimension to your life and boost your confidence level to great heights.

Chapter 6: Face Your Challenges Gracefully

70. Stamp Out Ageist Stereotypes

Although the term *ageism* can refer to prejudice against people in many different age groups, we commonly think of it in reference to older people. And no wonder. Perhaps no other segment of society finds itself stereotyped as widely as seniors, especially older women.

Even greeting card companies have gotten into the act of depicting older women as cantankerous and unwilling to bend. Many of us laugh at these cards, but when you think about it, they perpetuate the myth of the older woman as a wizened, rigid character who bosses people around like a dictator. She's old, she's entitled, and she's coming right at you whether you like it or not, they shout with their cartoon caricatures and snappy punch lines. In reality, we know that most older women display the opposite characteristics in that they're even-tempered, empathic, and considerate of others' feelings.

Have you spent time in a doctor's or dentist's office or a hospital where the staff infantilizes you by calling you by your first name? Somehow, it makes you feel more vulnerable and at their mercy instead of the equal that you are. If it bothers you, tell the office manager that you'd like everyone to refer to you as *Ms.*, *Miss,* or *Mrs.* and to please add that request to your records. The staff is usually happy to oblige, and if they don't, consider going elsewhere.

Similarly, people in many social situations talk down to older women by calling them *dear, honey*, or *sweetie*. Don't hesitate to tell the offenders that you'd prefer they call you by your given name or surname, and tell them what it is. By addressing an older person with these names, wait staff, salespeople, hospital, and retirement home personnel, among others, trivialize the women they think they're flattering.

You may love hearing one of these pet names from your partner, but hearing it from someone you'll never see again may seem like an insincere familiarity. I once heard a high school principal address female teachers as "girls," an inaccurate moniker since some of them were over 60. Although some older women may not find these terms offensive, others may find them patronizing and demeaning.

Some employers' ageist attitudes preclude them from hiring older, more experienced women. Although the law prohibits discrimination based on age, we know that these employers use criteria other than age to disqualify qualified older women from jobs they deserve.

What can you as an older woman do if you find someone talking down to you or making a joke at your expense? You can tell the person tactfully yet assertively that you don't appreciate the put-down or the joke. If the offender asks why, say that you don't believe that just because a woman's older, she should be treated with less respect than a younger person and that you'd appreciate it if he or she honors that in the future.

Of course, we'll never totally eradicate ageist stereotypes, but if we think about how it impacts our lives in our everyday interactions, and if we speak out against it, it's a good beginning.

71. Think of Your Age as an Asset

"When are you going to retire and start having fun?' my friends ask me. 'I am having fun working at a job I love,' I tell them with a smile, 'more fun than if I frittered away my days playing bingo and hanging out at the senior center like you old girls.' Of course, I envy them sometimes, but I say you should do whatever sets a fire under you. For me that's working at my own business."— 68-year-old costume jewelry store owner

Some women see their age as a liability instead of an asset. However, as we age, we have a lot more to offer the world and ourselves. For one thing, we see more ways to fix problems that come up in our lives and in the lives of those we care about. We know how to give advice, and if we don't have the answer, we say so. We're more honest and forthright with people without being unkind or hurtful.

Another plus advancing age brings us is a sense of what works and what doesn't in a variety of situations. We've been through so many struggles and predicaments that we're often able to advise ourselves and those we love about the best possible course of action in many situations. We know how to solve problems, how to mediate disputes, and how to come out on top of difficult circumstances with the least possible scarring of our and other people's psyches.

We're also more willing to listen and learn from others, without always thinking our way is best. Seeing all sides of a situation comes more easily now. Our egos don't intrude upon our judgment as they may once have done. We're able to weigh pros and cons and come up with a reasonable solution to our own problems and to those who seek our advice.

As older women, we've gained more confidence in ourselves, so that when we take our own advice or offer it to others, we don't second-guess ourselves. We've lived long enough to believe that the choices we make are good ones. We don't have to wonder and ruminate over which path to take because we've lived through similar situations before, and we have some sound ideas about how to proceed and progress in helping solve problems.

Best of all, we can think of our age as an asset because we don't play games as we may have in the past. We don't manipulate, put on airs, or pretend we're someone other than ourselves. We are who we are, and we're secure in who we choose to be. We see the benefits of being ourselves in all circumstances and know that not being true to ourselves can drag others and ourselves down. People seek our advice because they sense our authenticity and sincerity.

I've heard this same story from many different women. The words may differ, but the meaning's the same: "If only I knew then what I know now that I'm older. My marriage would have been more peaceful, my job less stressful, and my relationships more enjoyable." The best part of growing older is that our life experiences help us see things in a new light, with more patience and greater wisdom than we possessed in our younger years. Even though we brave many challenges as we age, for the most part we know better than at any other stage of life how to handle adversity. We also perceive more clearly what makes us happy and complete. And that's a plus.

72. Figure Out What's Holding You Back

There are so many things you want to do that you never had time for when you were caught up in the daily routines of work and family. Not that they weren't wonderful times, but you could barely catch up on what you had to do, let alone think about hobbies, time with friends, date nights, travel, or spending time developing a long-neglected talent. Now that you have the time to do the things you want, what's holding you back?

Many women are afraid of not succeeding at what they want most to do. Lack of motivation and, in some cases, lack of funds prevent women from taking the first step toward ensuring their fulfillment in life. Do you want to enjoy a favorite pastime? Talk yourself into starting it now. Do you want to plan the trip of your dreams but lack money? Search the Internet and talk to a travel agent.

Both are good sources of information to help you make your trip a reality by cutting a few corners even though you may think you can't afford it. Don't let fear hold you back. Most of the time, your fears are unfounded ideas you build up in your mind with no basis in fact. Some clear thinking on your part can help you eradicate them.

One of the strongest impediments to realizing your goals in retirement is the inability to get started. As you know, the hardest part of doing anything is making up your mind to commit to it by taking action. Try picking a day and a specific time to start doing what you want to do (making plans to meet a friend, redecorating your house, starting that new hobby you've always wanted to try, or writing that book), and indicate what you want to do on your calendar. Begin when you say you will. Promise yourself you'll stop procrastinating and give yourself the gift of doing something you value in a small or big way.

Do you sometimes think it's too late to do what you want to do? Here are some older women who refused to allow themselves to think that way. If they had, they would have never accomplished what some people call impossible. Look at this list, and remember that the number of women who have achieved great things later in life is limitless. Grandma Moses started painting at 75; Sue Monk Kidd published her first novel, *The Secret Life of Bees,* at 53; and Hedda Bolgar Bekker at age 102 worked as a psychologist in California. Who can forget Helen Hoover Santmyer who published her best-selling book, *And Ladies of the Club* at age 87?

Are other people's opinions holding you back from what you want to do? Sometimes well-meaning friends and relatives have a way of projecting their own beliefs onto others. Because they lack confidence or don't believe they could accomplish great things in their older years, they might tell you that you're not being realistic or that your beautiful dreams are merely pipe dreams. But you know better than to listen to advice like this. Stay clear of anyone who tells you you're too old, too tired, or totally impractical and that you should forget about doing the things you want. (Read more about these spoilers in Section 97, "Don't Let the Naysayers Get You Down.")

There's nothing holding you back but you. If you want something more, you can find it.

73. Turn Loneliness Around

"You'll never be lonely if you learn to befriend yourself."—Unknown

Some retired women I've talked to find themselves experiencing loneliness for the first time in their lives, and that's not surprising. For many years, we kept ourselves connected with a ready-made social network of our children and associates at work. People surrounded us most of the time, and we rarely felt lonely. On the other hand, we sometimes longed for time for ourselves, which we rarely got.

If loneliness bothers you sometimes, find a way to change that feeling into one of connection, friendship, and camaraderie. One simple thing you can do is call a friend; make a date for lunch or a movie. That's easy enough. If you'd like to go to a higher level and talk about your concerns with a friend you think feels the way you do, invite her over for lunch and ask for her suggestions about what she does when she feels lonely. Then reciprocate: Ask if anything's bothering her, and give her your best advice. Sometimes a soulful chat with a dear friend can leave you with usable ideas and go a long way in boosting your optimism. It also helps to know that other people have problems they grapple with. You're certainly not alone in feeling the way you do.

Another thing you may want to do to alleviate loneliness is to join or start a book club or discussion group. In addition to the intellectual stimulation such groups offer, you'll have the added benefit of spending an evening with like-minded people. If you're leaning toward a discussion group for retired women, you may want to focus on topics that concern all the participants: for example, problems that retired women endure like loneliness, fear, depression, boredom, and loss.

In another session you could discuss the positive side of retirement, which many women know outweighs the negative side. This might include: gaining more freedom and flexibility, exploring new hobbies and interests, embracing a more healthy lifestyle, and having more time to spend with your favorite people.

Focusing on others helps banish loneliness. One thing you can do is take a friend or relative under your wing, with the aim of improving this person's quality of life. Help someone solve a problem or advise him or her about something you're knowledgeable about so your friend or family member feels more secure in making a good decision.

Here's something else you can do: look in the newspaper for groups that share your interests who are looking for members. Churches and community organizations also sponsor these groups. If you'd like to join a specific activity, such as bowling, tennis, or golf, ask your friends if they know anyone looking for a partner, or join an established league. Morning mall walkers often share friendship while engaging in some rigorous exercise. There's something for everyone. All you have to do is find it. Before you know it, you'll have so many friends and new experiences, you'll wonder why you ever thought you were lonely.

Perhaps the best salve for loneliness is the advice in the quote that opens this section. Befriend yourself as you never have before. Enjoy your own company, and find activities to enlighten and amuse yourself. You're the best friend you'll ever have. Practice being friends with yourself, and you'll never feel alone again.

74. Face Your Fears Head On

"Never fear growing old; there are many who have never had the privilege."—Unknown

When you were busy at work or caring for your kids and the thousand other details of your life, your fears probably didn't seem as imposing. Maybe you've found that once you retired and didn't find yourself as overwhelmed with your daily schedule as you once were, you had more time to think about your fears. Little things that never bothered you before might affect you more deeply now.

You worry, sometimes excessively, about the health and safety of your partner, children, and grandchildren. You have more time to focus on your own health problems and may make them bigger than they are because you have more time to dwell on them. Even driving may make you more anxious in that you tend be more aware of other drivers who may be texting, talking on the phone, or driving recklessly. You find yourself driving more defensively, but you still wonder what you can do to help yourself and your passengers if a dangerous situation puts you off guard.

Little things that never bothered you can set your fear

barometer soaring. What kinds of things make you fearful? Many retired women are afraid of declining health. To combat these fears, keep yourself in the best shape possible, both physically and mentally. It's true that even if you do everything you can to ensure optimal health, illnesses may appear, but if that happens, you'll call up the strength to face it and adjust to it in the best possible way.

Many older women fear the unknown and ask themselves what will happen to them in the future. Will they have a strong support system if something goes wrong in their lives? Will they have enough money to last for the rest of their lives? They also think about the bigger questions such as "What happens after this life ends?"; "Does the spirit survive the body?"; and "What is the meaning of my existence?"

Sometimes, the more you ponder these questions, the harder it becomes to cope with the fears they engender in you. The best way to handle the more practical issues that relate to your health and well-being may be to do whatever you can to allay your fears about your future by preparing for it in the best way you can.

The deeper questions are, of course, harder to address. Turning to religion or your own brand of spirituality often helps calm your fears. However, we can never know all the answers about what happens after this life. While it may be fascinating and enlightening to speculate on these metaphysical questions, it's best not to ruminate on them to the extent that it interferes with your peace of mind.

A lot of older women fear losing their independence, and rightly so. That's why it's important to think about putting a plan into place before too many years elapse. If you don't want to depend on family members to care for you should you need extensive care, you'll need to think about what type of care you'd want if you find yourself in that predicament.

You don't have to do it immediately, but you should have an idea about what type of setting (individual or group) you'd prefer should you need it. You may also want to think about accident-proofing the home you currently live in to prevent falls. If you have any physical disabilities, you may want to invest in an alarm system that will contact help immediately should you require it.

Fears can cloud our thinking and deprive us of peace of mind. Do your best to look at your fears realistically. Talk to someone who understands and shares your fears. If you find they're more than you can bear, ask for help. You can overcome your fears.

75. Find Ways to Beat Feelings of Sadness

"Sadness flies away on the wings of time."—Jean de La Fontaine

Feelings of intense sadness, often in the form of a full-blown depression, hit retired women at double the rate men experience. That's not surprising because women frequently bear full responsibility for many major life decisions and take it upon themselves to solve everyone in the family's dilemmas, often single-handedly. Since women usually earn less than men, economic woes often cause them to feel a sense of uncertainty about the future. Women also are more likely to assume the role of primary caregiver for ailing parents and other family members.

How can you tell the difference between the feelings of sadness that hit retired women from time to time and a major depression? First of all, feelings of sadness are not nearly as intense, and they eventually pass, while depression manifests itself as a total lack of energy and the absence of a desire to do things you previously loved to do. Depressed people are more prone to ask themselves if their lives are worth living.

If you believe you're seriously depressed, see a doctor without delay. Request a physical to see if any physical causes would precipitate this major mood change. If you find that you are indeed depressed, seek help from a therapist.

It's normal for retired women to have occasional bouts of the blues. As a retiree, your life changes suddenly from fast-paced and regulated (you know what you have to do each day) to slower-paced (you're on your own now) with no particular routine to follow. You might find it taxing to be a self-starter, and that's where the idea of keeping a schedule for yourself helps (see Sections 13 and 14). You'll get used to the slower pace and settle into a routine if you give yourself time to get used to your new schedule.

Children leaving home can also provoke feelings of sadness. Of course, they usually leave for college or a job before you retire, but you may still feel that emptiness and sense of longing for them for years after they leave home. Conversely, maybe your children have returned home to live due to money problems. That can also make you sad because of the uncertainty of not knowing if and when they're going to venture out on their own. You've waited all this time to have time to yourself, and once again you're dealing with a full house.

Sure, you love your kids, but when will it be your time? Maybe you and your partner have gotten used to your privacy and freedom, and possibly, a revived love life, and now your life is back to the way it was. You're happy to help your children, and you would do anything for them, but you feel guilty for not always being enthusiastic about welcoming them, their laundry, and their friends. If you're feeling sad and discombobulated, don't berate yourself. Anyone would feel this ambivalence.

If you experience sadness once in a while, recognize the feeling and then do what you can to obliterate it. What's the use of wallowing in it? It doesn't get you anywhere and robs you of the happiness you deserve. It's your choice.

76. Build a Sense of Affiliation

One thing that women who worked outside their homes sorely miss is the sense of affiliation that their jobs afforded them. It's not only being part of an organization, a company, or a group of work associates, but rather an entire network of friendships you've made and nourished over the years. The people you ate lunch with and shared stories with gave you that sense of connection. Moreover, your conversations with work friends also provided you with intellectual stimulation and the chance to share ideas, opinions, jokes, recipes, and sometimes, good food. And don't forget about the parties in and outside of your workplace. For the most part, you shared a bond like no other with your work colleagues.

Even if you disliked your job, you probably enjoyed the socializing and sense of companionship and that "we're in this together" feeling that socializing with your work buddies gave you. When you retire, that sense of affiliation leaves you, and you'll want to find something to fill the void.

Whether you were a single working person or combined work with raising your children, that sense of connection with your work associates filled the important need of granting you a built-in social network. It doesn't matter whether you associated with all or only one of your colleagues: you shared conversations, laughs, and sometimes problems.

If you stayed home to raise your children, you also built a sense of affiliation. You saw your kids every day, and you had a routine that centered around them. You also networked with other mothers, arranged play dates, helped one another in emergencies, and discussed your concerns about your family life with one another. You enjoyed a strong sense of affiliation, which may now no longer be part of your life. You, like those who worked outside their homes, may sorely miss it.

Here are some ideas to recoup that feeling you got from being a part of something that was more important than the job itself. Consider going out with one or more of your favorite relatives or friends on a regular basis.

Find a movie, museum, or concert that all of you will enjoy, one that you can discuss afterwards. You may want to attend the theater and see a favorite play. Make it a day, starting with a train ride so that no one has to put up with the hassles of driving, then going to a restaurant (take turns choosing one) before or after the show, and finally, seeing a matinee, usually at a better price than you'd find at prime time. Making time to engage in these activities regularly will grant you the camaraderie and a mental shot in the arm similar to, and maybe even better than, the one you got from spending time with your work companions.

You may also want to think about going on an outing sponsored by your local community or church. Dinner theater trips, shows, and cruises often appear in their list of offerings. These trips can help you meet a new circle of friends and provide you with hours of entertainment and good company.

Did you ever think of working for the political party of your choice? You could do a great service by helping to get out the vote while promoting the candidate you believe could best do the job. As a bonus, you'll meet people who share your opinions and you'll be working for a cause you believe in.

Once you've left your job, building your own sense of affiliation will help make the transition from the workplace to your new life easier and less traumatic. Brainstorm some of your own ideas to recapture this most gratifying side of your job. It will prove the best of both worlds: you'll enjoy friendship, give your brain a boost with good conversation, and go to places you wouldn't have a chance to enjoy if you were still working. The best part is that you won't have to put up with any of the negative aspects that made your job less than perfect.

77. Stay in Touch with Loved Ones Near and Far

"Don't allow the grass to grow on the path of friendship."—Native American Proverb

While you were working on the job or raising your family or doing both, you probably found it impossible to find time for visits with people you care about most. Now that you're retired, you have more time. All you have to do is find ways to keep in touch with the people you cherish.

Make the resolution to stay in touch with the most important people in your life, whether they live close by or far away. Find a unique and novel way to do this, one you like doing, and you'll be more apt to stay connected. You can also take the more comfortable route and set a time to talk every week by phone so that every week at the same time you'll count on talking to your parent, aunt, or sister who lives relatively close by or to your long-time neighbor who moved to the opposite coast. Also, you can keep in touch by e-mail, and the person you write to can answer at his or her convenience. Texting is much less personal, don't you think? It's good for short messages but lacks the personal touch of a phone call or letter.

Speaking of letters, you may want to buy some pretty stationary and use a favorite pen to compose a letter to that person you're missing. Nothing touches someone like getting a letter that you took the time to write and send. Tell your friends or relatives how much they mean to you and that you've been thinking about them a lot. Ask them to write back, and don't be surprised if they do. Writing letters may be old-fashioned, but this type of correspondence never goes out of style. Handwritten letters provide a proven way of telling someone they're important to you. If handwriting poses a problem for you, type your letters on a computer.

If you want to communicate a high tech way, try a video chat. You can hear each other's voices and see the face of a special person in your life that you may not have visited with in a long time.

Have you ever thought about planning a family reunion? Of course, you'd have to ask for help from other family members. It usually takes a year to plan such an event. First you have to decide on a location, which is usually centrally situated. Find a venue you know everyone will love, perhaps a shore or mountain setting or a park that boasts many activities for the different age groups in attendance.

Each person on the reunion committee assumes responsibility for a specific task such as location, activities, and food. You can also ask someone to act as the official photographer who will record your special event for posterity. That person can send photos via the Internet to all the participants.

A regularly scheduled event that brings everyone together like few others is the traditional Sunday dinner. Many years ago, the Sunday dinner tradition started in England, and it's been going strong ever since. Family members usually meet earlier than the dinner hour, often between 12:00 and 2:00 PM at one person's house each Sunday for food, conversation, and possibly a few games that people of all ages can play. You can rotate the dinner location if you want, and if one person doesn't relish the idea of doing all the work, each person can bring a certain type of food (main dish, salad, or dessert) to complete the feast.

For as long as I can remember, we gathered at my mother's cozy ranch house to enjoy sumptuous meals of pasta, salad, and elaborate desserts like strawberry shortcake. We'd talk about our lives and debate national affairs long into the afternoon. After dinner, the children gathered in Mom's spacious backyard, playing ball and hide and seek. I never forgot those dinners and the sense of closeness they engendered in our family. Think about starting your own Sunday dinner tradition. You can hold it at whatever interval you choose: weekly, bi-monthly, or monthly.

It doesn't take much effort to stay in touch with the people we care about most. Find a way that pleases you, and start calling, writing, video chatting or planning a Sunday dinner, and you're on your way.

78. Cope with Losses in Your Life

"Mostly it is loss which teaches us about the worth of things."—Arthur Schopenhauer

As we grow older, we accrue many benefits that we didn't enjoy in our working years. We're grateful for our new freedom and the chance to get involved in activities and adventures we didn't have time for earlier. We enjoy charting our grandkids' development as they mature into young men and women. If we don't have kids or grandkids, we're watching our lives unfold with more happiness and adventure than they ever did before. Whatever our situations, we're living the best time of our lives, and we're living more intensely than we did at any other stage of our existence.

However, the reality is that gains we're now realizing are, at times, offset by the losses that come our way. It's painful to experience loss at any age, but at this time in our lives, we often feel more vulnerable and more deeply affected by losses. However, we can find ways to cope and not let the distress we suffer destroy our chance for happiness.

Smaller losses are, of course, more manageable. Many women find the aging process frustrating and lament what they perceive as losing the attractiveness, charm, and desirability they once had. They're upset about weight gain or loss, hair thinning, and skin changes. But we know we can look attractive at any age if we take care of our bodies and maximize our assets with cosmetics and the right clothes. In the final analysis, we know that attractiveness is more than our physical appearance. Remaining active and vital go a long way toward giving us a youthful glow, more than any makeover could possibly offer.

Loss of the ability to do things you once did or the slowing down of your pace is another problem that often frustrates retired women. Many retired women display more energy than their younger friends and can still play a rigorous game of tennis or dance into the wee hours. However, for those who don't have the energy level they once boasted, adjusting to a more relaxed pace can prove daunting.

Sometimes health problems such as arthritis, hip or knee issues, hearing or vision loss, or chronic pain can precipitate the need to slow down. Whatever the reason, find out what you can do to alleviate your health problems and then decide to do the best with what you have. You can still live an active, productive life with a few modifications.

One of the biggest losses we can suffer during these years is the loss of our parents. No matter how old they are, it's still gut-wrenching to accept the reality that they will no longer be with us. At the same time, we may lose some of our other family members who have figured prominently in our lives since our childhood days. When we lose these dear ones, we feel that we've lost part of our history, who we are, and where we came from. Very often the worst part of losing those we love comes in small ways, which can be even harder to live with than the strong waves of sadness that invariably hit us when we least expect it.

Sometimes we'll reach for the phone to call the person we lost and then realize she won't be there to answer. Loss of family members and close friends often cause us more sadness on holidays, birthdays, and occasions when we regularly gathered to celebrate.

Coping with losses in our lives, particularly the monumental ones, is the biggest challenge we'll ever take on. Therefore, we need to search for ways to deal positively with these voids in our lives. When we make this effort, we'll begin to see that we have more strength and courage than we thought we could call forth despite the enormity of our losses.

79. Treasure Memories of Loved Ones

"Though nothing can bring back the hour of splendor in the grass, of glory in the flower, we will grieve not, rather find strength in what remains behind."—William Wordsworth

Losing someone you love is the hardest blow life will deal you. You will never forget that person who made a deep impression on your life, whether it's your parent, dear relative, or a devoted friend. It's a fact that grief can last for months, and even years. If you believe your profound sense of sorrow is lasting longer than you think it should, be sure to consult a therapist.

However, if you believe you can manage those feelings of sorrow on your own, it helps to attend a support group such as one offered by a faith community or hospital. Some funeral homes also offer these groups. Hospices are an excellent resource for grief support even if you haven't used their services. Some people prefer online support groups, but be sure that they function under the direction of a trained counselor.

In addition to joining a support group, here are some suggestions for things you can do to help yourself through these trying periods. Keep your loved ones alive by joining with other family members in remembering them. Peruse photos of them with others who knew them, and recreate memories of the events these photos bring to mind.

Share anecdotes about the person who meant so much to you. You may not have heard a certain story before, and it will offer a fresh revelation into the person's life and make how much that person meant to you more tangible. Telling old stories and hearing new ones will perpetuate the beautiful memories your loved one has given you and others.

Something else you can do to keep your relative's or friend's memory alive is to wear jewelry that person bought for you. Along the same lines, if someone has bequeathed jewelry to you, it may give you a sense of closeness with your loved one even though that person is no longer here. Some people believe that jewelry carries a person's emotional vibrations. Wearing jewelry given to you as a gift or handed down by a loved one can sometimes help you feel that person's presence if you are sensitive that way. Try it and see.

Some people who want to memorialize a person find it comforting to set up a memorial in the corner of a room, using a small table to display pictures and other mementoes. This helps them think of the person every time they walk by. If you've inherited a piece of furniture from your loved one, you can use that as a display table.

So many of our memories revolve around food and conviviality with those we hold dear. Cook recipes you learned from the person you want to remember or recipes they often made for themselves and others. Often, certain smells evoke memories more than those engendered by any other senses. When you smell food cooking that your loved one often cooked (be it pot roast, pasta, or chocolate cake), it resurrects happy memories and helps that person live on in your mind. Invite other family members to enjoy that special food with you and have fun reminiscing.

On your loved one's birthday, hold a small celebration to remember him or her. Cook something tasty you used to eat with that person or one you know they enjoyed. Make it simple, but make it your best. Brew some coffee or tea and enjoy a dessert celebration. Maybe the person loved cheesecake, blueberry pie, or an orange cake that she invented. Sit around the table with others who knew the person and let it be known that this happy celebration is held in memory of (Mom, Grandmom, Dad, or a friend). All present can share a happy memory of the person they have loved and lost.

Think of a way to remember one who has gone before that you deeply loved. You'll enjoy it, as will those who join in the celebration. And possibly the person you're remembering will too. You never know.

80. Seek Help If You Need It

"Ask, and it shall be given you, seek, and ye shall find; knock, and it shall be opened unto you."—Matthew 7:7, *King James Bible*

At any age, problems can pile up, overwhelming us at times. Disappointments, losses, and family problems beset us, sometimes when we least expect them. You can face your challenges and learn to cope with them if you're willing to ask for help when you need it. If your problem isn't overwhelming, talk to someone you're close to and enjoy a good rapport with about it.

Before you begin to reach out to someone about your problem, think about the advice this person gave you in the past. Did you find it beneficial, or did it fail to help you progress in finding a solution to your problem? Be sure to choose the right person to confide in and one that you can trust not to betray your confidence to others. Also, opt for someone who will be objective and one who will not overplay or underplay your problem. Explain to your confidant what's bothering you, and talk about any physical and psychological symptoms you're experiencing. Listen with an open mind to the suggestions the person offers. Then determine whether you'd feel comfortable following the advice. In the end, of course, you'll make the final decision based on your own best judgment about which course to take.

Make it a point to write in your journal, no holds barred, about the issues causing you emotional pain and turmoil. Look at what you wrote, and gauge the seriousness of the issues you're dealing with and your response to them.

Determine what type of action on your part your reactions warrant: talking to someone you believe you can confide in or seeking specialized help in the form of therapy. If issues that come up in your life appear so severe that you can't handle them alone, or if talking to a friend or relative doesn't seem to alleviate the problem, ask your doctor for a referral to a psychologist or psychiatrist who will treat you with psychotherapy and medication, should you need it. If you decide on therapy, but think it's beyond your financial reach (sadly, many senior health plans don't reimburse for therapy), go to someone who accepts a sliding scale based on income or to a community agency, which often charges lower rates.

If you do choose the therapy route, talk freely to your therapist regarding your feelings about medications. Become a partner in your health care as you will whenever you have any physical or psychological problem. If you don't feel that the course of treatment is helping you, discuss your concerns with the therapist. If you cannot come to an agreement, seek help elsewhere.

Some older women believe that asking for help for problems shows weakness on their part. These women were taught from an early age to believe that it's important to solve their own problems and that asking for help is a last resort only applicable in serious cases of mental illness. Happily, these attitudes are changing, and women have realized that seeking help is the right thing to do if they find their problems difficult to solve on their own.

Whether you seek the advice of a friend or look for professional help in dealing with your problem, you'll be glad you met your challenges head on and did your part to find a solution that allows you to live your life in the best way possible without undue stress and tension.

81. Look For a Support Group

"The feeling of having shared in a common peril is one element in the powerful cement which binds us."—Alcoholics Anonymous: The Big Book

In addition to discussing problems, losses, and disappointments with a trusted friend or therapist, look for support groups in your area that offer help with a variety of challenges such as drug and alcohol addiction, physical disabilities, grief, and other physical and mental health issues. You can find advice and support from peers and a group leader about any of these issues for yourself or a family member. Access information about support groups online, and the organization will refer you to a local chapter.

You'll want to look at the philosophy and mission statement of the group to determine if it's consistent with your own beliefs and value system. If you find the philosophical underpinnings of the organization something that would not fit in with your own ideas, look for a different group. You'll find many that address the same issues.

If you're dealing with problems of aging relatives, most communities have an agency for the elderly that will help you locate assisted living facilities or nursing homes. Look online under *Council on Aging* to find ones in your state and neighborhood. For more information about this and other groups that help older people, see Section 90, "Volunteer to Assist Older People."

If there's a topic you'd like to explore and discuss with others in your situation and you can't find a support group that addresses your problem, you have the option of forming your own support group. If you know two or more women experiencing a similar problem, plan to meet with them periodically to brainstorm and exchange ideas to help one another address problems related to the issues you're facing.

Whether you decide to seek an established support group or form your own, take the time to evaluate how much the support group is helping you. If you have concerns, talk to the group leader if you're in a regular support group. If, after a few sessions, you find the group is not helping, look for another one. The rapport and focus of the group has to be right for each person in the group for it to work. Assess how it's working for you, and proceed from there.

These days support groups exist for every problem you can think of, and they're willing to help you find a way to cope with your challenges in the best way possible. Support groups are as close as your local newspaper or your computer. Why not take advantage of the expertise and peace of mind they offer?

82. Put Your Challenges in Perspective

"I've had a few hardships in my life: losing the man I loved and lived with for 52 years, losing my best friend, and losing my ability to get around like I used to. But the worst thing that can ever happen to you is losing hope. I never lost that. I always wake up happy I'm alive and raring to go on."—78-year-old retired social worker

Most women will tell you that their life in retirement brings them more happiness than they could have imagined. You have the freedom to do what you want when you want, and engaging hobbies and good company give you a full and active life, one that you never experienced before.

At every stage of life you've dealt with challenges, but you always got through them as you will now. What can you do to put your challenges in perspective so that you will not feel overpowered by them when they come your way? For one thing, you can list in your journal many of the positive things that have happened in your life in recent years. For this exercise, you may want to consider the past five or ten years. Go back even further if you like.

After stating the positive experiences, write your reaction to these events that buoyed you up. What did you do to help make them happen, or were they things that happened in the natural course of events? What did you gain from them? Why are they memorable? Also, list the challenges you've dealt with within that time span. Tell how you've coped with them. How did you change because of them? Finally, what have you learned because of the positive and negative life events that marked these years?

Another thing you can do to put your challenges in perspective is to write a short journal entry or a poem about what you most look forward to in the future. How does what you want to do link with what you've learned from your experiences in the past? How much did both the gratifying and difficult events in your life impact what you happily anticipate for your future? How did both types of events mold you into who you are today and who you aspire to be tomorrow? Address all of these questions in your journal or poem.

Here's something else you can do to put balance in your life, especially when your challenges dominate your thinking and overshadow the good things happening around you. Think about the people and events that inspire gratitude in you. Focus on your blessings rather than on the problems and pitfalls you encounter.

You can also find your own unique ways to overcome obstacles that pull you down and make you forget about the happy times. Once you find an individual way to address your feelings about your challenges, put your plan in motion. Believe that you are stronger than any challenges you meet and that you will find a way to deal with them so they don't take over your life. Believe and it will happen.

Chapter 6: Takeaways

- Speak out against ageist treatment from professionals, service people, and others.

- Don't let anyone (including yourself) hold you back from accomplishing what you want to do.

- Find a way to change feelings of loneliness into feelings of connection, friendship, and camaraderie.

- View your fears realistically.

- Determine the difference between feelings of sadness and a major depression.

- Find something to fill the void when you lose your sense of affiliation from being a working single person or an employed or stay-at-home mother.

- Resolve to stay in touch with the most important people in your life whether they live close by or far away.

- Find ways to cope with losses, and don't let the distress you feel from them hurt your chances for happiness.

- Think of ways to memorialize a person that you deeply loved and lost.

- Be willing to ask for help from a friend, professional, or support group when you need it.

- Believe that you are stronger than any challenges you face.

Quiz #5: Face Your Challenges Gracefully

While retirement features many happy tines, it also brings challenges. What's important is how you go about facing the challenges that this stage of life brings. What helps you most when dealing with issues that concern you? Take the quiz to get an idea of your ability to cope with challenges in a positive, constructive manner.

1. If personnel in a medical office call you by your first name,

    a) don't say anything. They're trying to help you relax by acting friendly.

    b) ask them to refer to you as *Ms., Miss,* or *Mrs.,* along with your surname, whichever you prefer.

c) tell them you love it. Hearing yourself called by your first name makes you feel like a sprightly, young chick.

2. One of the worst impediments to helping you realize your goals in retirement is

a) that you're busy with a hundred other things.

b) the inability to get started.

c) the feeling that you'll never accomplish them, so why try?

3. The best antidote for loneliness is to

a) surround yourself with people every waking moment.

b) befriend yourself as you never have before.

c) spend at least two hours a day using social media to connect with friends.

4. If you feel temporary sadness (not depression), once in a while,

a) don't bother to acknowledge it. It will leave as quickly as it came.

b) recognize the feeling, and do what you can to overcome it.

c) plan a wild bash with your friends at the local saloon.

5. After you leave your job, building a sense of affiliation will

a) help you make new friends.

b) make the transition from the workplace to your new life easier and less traumatic.

c) keep you so busy socializing you'll wish you'd stayed in your job.

6. When you're trying to stay in touch with friends and family, nothing affects them like

a) finding an e-mail from you in their in-box.

b) getting a letter you wrote in your own handwriting mailed to them.

c) getting a message from you on their social media site.

7. The key to dealing with loss lies in

a) telling ourselves there's nothing we can do about it, so we need to adjust to it in the best way we can.

b) finding ways to deal positively with these voids in our lives.

c) allowing ourselves to have a good cry and then moving on to an enjoyable activity.

8. How does cooking recipes handed down by our loved ones help memorialize them?

a) It makes us remember how hard they worked to make great meals for us.

b) It helps us retrieve happy memories from the aromas of the food we shared with them.

c) It makes us recall how they were able to cook without a recipe and how much we need one to make the recipe turn out right.

9. You can face your challenges and deal with them if

a) you keep telling yourself that this too shall pass.

b) you're willing to ask for help when you need it.

c) you don't dare ask for help because people will see you as a weakling.

10. Before you join a support group,

a) think about what people would think if they saw you going there.

b) consider the group's philosophy and mission statement to see if it's consistent with your beliefs.

c) check out the other members of the group to see if they seem like people you'd go out with socially.

11. When your challenges dominate your thinking, it helps to

a) put them out of your mind. Thinking about them will make you more anxious.

b) focus on people and events that inspire gratitude in you.

c) take your mind off them by shopping until you drop.

Answers

Mostly A's: If you want to face your challenges gracefully, look more closely at the variety of options at your disposal to solve the major and minor problems bothering you. Take control of your life by looking for solutions and implementing them. You are more powerful than you think.

Mostly B's: You're taking positive steps to face your challenges gracefully. You try to face your problems head on and look for viable solutions to address them. Your strength in times of trouble will help you get through any difficulties that cross your path.

Mostly C's: Don't worry about what other people think as you try to find constructive ways to address your problems. Concentrate on facing your challenges rather than avoiding thinking about them. Once you make a stronger effort to acknowledge your challenges and make the commitment to look for solutions, you'll be on your way.

Chapter 7: Live a Meaningful Life

83. What Does "The Good Life" Mean to You?

"If you ask me what I came to do in this word, I will tell you, I came to live out LOUD."—Emile Zola

What does the expression "The Good Life" mean to you? We've come a long way from Aristotle's definition of a "good life." He believed that the good life dealt mainly with the activity of the soul in connection with virtue. Most of us women, on the other hand, believe that the good life means living the life that's important to us as individuals.

For many of us that includes finding the most happiness we can muster in our daily lives by loving and being loved by family and friends. It means helping one another thrive and survive. It also means living a virtuous life (you got this one right, Aristotle) where we not only show concern for the people in our lives but for all of humanity.

Given the times, you're probably not surprised to know that Aristotle also believed that women, in addition to those he thought of as lower segments of society, could not live the good life because they couldn't decide things for themselves or choose an action for its own sake. This, in his view, made them unable to practice the virtues.

One thing we know for sure is that Aristotle (even though he came from a different era) didn't speak for today's women when he said that we could not live the good life. If we had lived during those times, I like to think we would surely have risen up in rebellion.

Before you can live "the good life," you have to decide what these words mean to you personally. Here are some things you can do to shape your thoughts into words. In your journal, brainstorm words and phrases that you'd associate with "the good life." Based on your brainstorming ideas, write a few sentences defining "the good life." Does it mean a happy and harmonious family life, good health, comfortable finances, or all of the above? What else does it mean to you personally? If one of these elements were missing, would you still characterize your life as good? Now try to encapsulate your definition of what the good life means to you in one sentence.

Here's something else you can do to pinpoint your definition of the good life. Invite two or three thinking friends over for a philosophical discussion of "the good life." Prepare a simple lunch, snacks, or buy take-out. Spend time discussing and debating your perceptions of "the good life." Have each person give examples from her own life. Discuss whether we as women have come full circle in having the capacity to live the life of our dreams, the best life possible. After listening to each other's ideas, claim as your own the ones that appeal most to you. Later, add them to the definition you wrote in your journal.

Think about the final version of your definition. To what extent are you living your best life possible? Are you living your life out loud as Zola lived his?

84. Examine Your Belief Systems

"Every mental act is composed of doubt and belief, but it is belief that is the positive, it is belief that sustains thought and holds the world together."—Soren Kierkegaard

As many of us reach this stage of our lives, we begin to ask ourselves in earnest the deeper questions: Who am I? Where am I headed? What do I hold true? Maybe we've asked ourselves these questions at major turning points in our lives such as during our teenage years and after graduation from high school and college, but at no other time did they prompt us to address them with such intensity as they do now. Some women fear exploring or questioning their belief systems, but those who dare often find the process rewarding and enlightening.

In your journal, record the deeper questions that you wonder about most. Take your time answering them so that you reflect your thoughts as accurately as possible. When you finish, write a statement that shows your basic philosophy of life. Discuss it with a friend and compare notes with what she believes.

If you belong to a religious institution, do you believe its basic tenants with the same fervor you felt in your younger days? Naturally, as the years go by, many women change or modify their ideas about their beliefs, and there's nothing disloyal or problematic about that. Healthy questioning can actually make you stronger and more faithful in your beliefs, or it could precipitate a change. When we become complacent and don't question our beliefs and the institutions we support, we sometimes find ourselves wondering if we're acting true to ourselves by remaining in them.

Think about what you like and dislike about your religious affiliation if you have one. Given any dissatisfactions you have, do you believe you'd feel comfortable enough to remain in it, or do you believe you need to make a change? Conversely, if you firmly believe in the ideas your church promotes and wouldn't think of changing, how can you enhance your religious beliefs to optimize your experience in your congregation ?

The same need to evaluate and modify your political beliefs holds true. Do you believe in your party's platform strongly enough to support its candidates in every election? Conversely, would you prefer to vote for a candidate rather than a specific platform? If so, maybe declaring yourself an independent would prove a better course to take.

What is your thinking about the controversial subjects that confront all of us on a national and international level? Have you changed or modified your thinking about them, or do you still hold the same positions you held in the past? It's helpful to re-think your stance on different social issues to determine whether you still feel the same way. These beliefs feed into political and religious beliefs, so it's helpful to reevaluate them every so often.

If we begin to examine our broader belief systems, first by asking ourselves the questions at the beginning of this section, this will lead us to an assessment of our convictions about politics, religion, and our opinions about social issues in our own world and in society at large. Doing this helps us remain young and vital in our thoughts. The more we consider our belief systems, modifying or changing them as we think best, the better off we will fare as women in our communities, our nation, and our world.

85. Find Ways to Explore Your Spirituality

"There are more things in heaven and earth, Horatio, than are dreamt of in your philosophy."—Hamlet, Shakespeare

If you feel compelled to explore your spirituality in ways other than those presented by your religious beliefs, you'll find many alternatives. More than a few organized religions frown upon such spiritual paths because they believe that so-called "New Age" ideas contradict their teachings. However, some women believe that other paths to spirituality can actually enhance their religious beliefs. As always, you decide.

If you'd like to learn more about getting in touch with your higher self, you may want to research ways of developing your sixth sense. Part of this process involves learning about clairvoyance (psychic knowing), clairsentience (psychic touch or feeling), and clairaudience (psychic hearing). Whenever you do any kind of psychic work, remember that it's very important to ask God, or whatever higher source you believe in, for protection and to surround yourself with the white light so that you attract only good.

All of us possess innate intuitive talents to one degree or another. You've probably had episodes in which you knew who was calling before you heard the person's voice or when you knew something was going to happen before it materialized. Most of us have also experienced thinking about a relative or friend and then getting a call or an e-mail from that person. We've all encountered episodes that point to the fact that we are more than the sum total of our five senses. We are all intuitive whether we want to acknowledge it or not.

Most psychics possess strong abilities in one or more of the areas listed. You can find out more about enhancing and using your psychic abilities by taking online courses or by taking a course at a local night school or community college.

Would you like to learn more about angels and how they can help protect and guide you? As a starting point, read Dr. Doreen Virtue's books. Many women believe that angels are always close by, protecting them from physical and psychological danger. You may want to tap into angel power to guide you.

Prayer has also been proven to help people beat illnesses and heal more quickly. Use your own words or traditional prayers to boost your healing power. Also, learning about alternative healing modalities can help you and others enjoy better health. Reiki and other forms of energy healing spring from the natural ability we all have to optimize the way we feel in mind and body. Many hospitals (even those sponsored by organized religions) offer healing energy before and after surgery and provide it as an adjunct to treatments for various illnesses, including cancer.

If you feel comfortable exploring your spirituality in some of these ways and you can reconcile doing so with your religious belief system, by all means learn as much as you can and see where it leads you. It's your choice.

86. Delve into Self-Help Books

There's a self-help book for everyone. What areas of life do you find causes you pain or problems? Over the years, the same issues may resurface and others may take their place. Whether your problems dominate your life or cause mild aggravation, finding an authoritative self-help book written by an expert can present a positive first step in discovering practical solutions that will substantially improve your life.

How do you know if you can depend on the information offered in the self-help book you're thinking about reading? When you read a book, a newspaper, a magazine article, or hear a TV or radio broadcast, you always need to consider the reliability of the information. It helps to learn about the author's or broadcaster's biases, political orientation, and philosophy of life. It's also important to determine if the writer or broadcaster possesses the proper credentials academically and also in the area of life experience.

Another thing to consider when you choose a self-help book is writing style and voice. Do you prefer an academic treatment of the subject with a more technical vocabulary or a more hands-on practical approach that also gives you information you can count on but in a more conversational manner? What type of writing style rivets you to the page? Mainly, what do you want to take away from the book? Look at the blurb on the back of the book and the table of contents to determine if the book contains the specific information you're seeking.

Ask friends, your librarian, and bookseller for recommendations for books in your area of interest. Once you find self-help authors whose books you enjoy reading, study their websites and blogs to gain more information, which, in turn, will give you even more sources to consult to help you expand your knowledge of the topic.

You can see from looking at the number of self-help books in your library and bookstore that it's one of the most popular types of book published. Women want answers to their problems, and self-help books are an excellent place to start looking for them. They will give you many usable ideas about where to find help and make you know that you're not alone. Once you know that others share your problem and that with some effort you will find a resolution, you'll have hope that whatever's troubling you will eventually come to an end. Hope is the beginning of healing.

87. Study Inspirational Books, Blogs, and Social Media Sites

"You can't wait for inspiration. You have to go after it with a club."—Jack London

Inspirational books, blogs, and social media sites can help you get a handle on any problems or dilemmas you confront. Inspirational books or motivational books, like self-help books, assist you in helping yourself, with the added benefit of giving you a call to action so that you can motivate yourself to learn what's preventing you from living your best life possible.

To find these books, look in a search engine by typing in the words *inspirational books.* If you're seeking one on a specific topic, add that word too. These books come in prose or poetry form and usually provide easy reading on deep subjects. Often, they chronicle a person's struggles and triumphs over adversity, providing a captivating and engaging story from which you can take away valuable life lessons.

Some of these books provide a road map for living your best life possible in a way that will motivate and inspire you. Inspirational books run the gamut from classics like *The Diary of Anne Frank* and *The Power of Positive Thinking* to contemporary books such as *The Alchemist, The Last Lecture, The Secret*, and *The Four Agreements.*

Other types of non-fiction books you'll find inspiring consist solely of poetry, quotations, or art. Perusing any of these inspirational books can transform your irritable mood into a happy one or a lazy day into a productive one. After a session reading poetry or quotations, try composing your own poetry or quotations about how to enhance meaning and satisfaction in your life as a retiree. You can also present one or more of your own creations to a friend or relative in your own handwriting on decorated stationary as a uniquely personal gift that the recipient will cherish as a keepsake for years to come.

Borrow books containing inspiring art from your favorite masters from the library or purchase them. Looking at these art books can help sharpen your sense of how much beauty exists in the world and give you a needed break from your daily routine. Books featuring works of art can also provide a spark to ignite your own creative abilities such as writing, art, crafting, or flower arranging.

Art books provide a starting point for conversation among your children, other family members, and friends. Browse the paintings together and ask: Why do you think the artist used the colors she did to paint the sunset (flowers, fruit, etc.)? What does the body language of the people in the painting tell you about what the people are thinking? What does it say about how they feel about one another?

Looking at art books with grandchildren can be an enlightening experience for them and you, sharpening their and your aesthetic senses, but most of all, bringing you closer together. Keep the questions simple, and they'll surprise you with their perceptive answers. Here are some sample questions you can use as starting points for discussion: What does the painting mean to you? What do you think the people in the painting are saying to one another? How do the colors make you feel? If you were painting a picture like this, what colors would you use and why?

You may also want to look up blogs and social media features like Pinterest, which offer many elevating thoughts that will provide you with hours of inspiration and motivation in the form of poems, quotes, sayings, and art. Plug whatever you're seeking inspiration for into a search engine and find a treasure trove of helpful advice.

Inspirational books, blogs, and social media sites can give you a lift when you're feeling low, motivate you when you're lacking energy, and help you rise above your problems, whatever they may be.

88. Find Opportunities to Practice Compassion and Empathy

"When I'm listening, really listening, with my ears, eyes, and heart to someone telling me a story about their lives, I feel it's such a close connection that I can reach out and touch that person's soul."—Rhonda, 60-year-old hospice nurse

Many medical authorities tell us that practicing compassion and empathy helps improve our physical and emotional health while helping others by caring about them and giving them our full attention. Every day brings us more opportunities to show compassion to those we know both intimately and casually. When we show compassion, we acknowledge and share our concern for other people's suffering.

Showing empathy means putting ourselves in another's situation and feeling exactly what that person feels so that we can help him or her in the best possible way. When displaying empathy, we are able to "read" people to learn exactly what they're feeling, and we fully grasp the depths of their discontent and pain. At other times, we may experience the full impact of their joyful experiences.

Many opportunities present themselves to practice compassion when we see relatives and friends going through traumatic life events, such as divorce, a death in the family, or a job loss. We can reach out to them by providing creature comforts like food and babysitting services, or by helping maintain their households by doing chores and errands to help make their lives more comfortable.

We also show compassion to people we know or to people we've heard about in the news who are suffering by assisting them with emotional support, financial help, or donations of food and clothing. Sometimes you'll see a friend or acquaintance asking for moral support on social media. A few kind words can go a long way and lift that person up when she's feeling low. When a group of people offer kind words and suggestions to someone on a public forum, the person processes it as a warm show of support, a cyber group hug, if you will.

Most women are adept at reading non-verbal signals. After all, we've had years of practice with our partners, kids, friends, and co-workers, who always came to us first when trouble struck. Tuning in to these signals helps us build a stronger rapport with those we're helping. It also helps us understand the full extent of people's problems when we actively listen to what they say. In line with this, we can show empathy by truly being there for those we care about and listening more than talking when they need our full attention. We can show our concern by offering our best response after tuning into their feelings with our empathic sense.

Consider how you can find opportunities to show compassion and empathy to others. Help change the lives of those you care about and, as a bonus, reap benefits for yourself in the form of enhanced health and happiness.

89. Mentor Others with Your Knowledge

"To the world you may just be somebody, but to somebody, you may just be the world."—Unknown

In Section #65, Showcase Your Talents, we discussed finding a mentor, someone to help you learn more about your areas of interest so that you can blossom and thrive. Have you ever considered mentoring someone and giving her the benefit of your knowledge and expertise? Mentoring could prove to be one of the most enriching experiences of your life.

Many organizations, such as Big Sisters, provide mentoring opportunities. In this organization, for example, you help guide a young woman (ages 6-18) though her journey to a well-adjusted, happy adulthood with your sage advice, steady support, and dependable friendship.

Look in an online search engine under *mentoring organizations* to find descriptions of this and other mentoring organizations in your area. Your local newspaper and Chamber of Commerce also list them. In addition to contacting organizations sponsoring mentoring opportunities, you can also mentor a friend, family member, or neighbor who would like to embrace a career or interest similar to yours. In this case, you don't have to attend meetings or join a group. All that's required is to make yourself available for phone calls and e-mails when the person you're helping needs guidance about her job, interests, or hobbies.

Say you've worked in management. Volunteer to help someone starting out in the field by offering suggestions about dealing with personnel in a positive way to get the best results, and address methods of solving workplace conflicts and other concerns as they come up on the job.

Likewise, if you were a teacher, you may know a neighbor's child who is studying education or who's launching a career in teaching. Guide the aspiring or new teacher with valuable information you've gleaned over the years about teaching methods, disciplinary techniques, and the best way to conduct a parent/teacher conference. Consider what you've learned from your years in the classroom as you advise the prospective or new teacher. What would you do again, and what would you change?

Consider this mentoring opportunity: Some of your neighbors may not have their families living nearby and may need someone like you as a resource person to help address problems they run into raising their children. Whether you stayed home to raise your kids or combined work with motherhood, offer to mentor new parents.

Your invaluable experience will help them cope with infant sleep problems, a toddler's incessant "no," and teenage angst and rebelliousness. You can be the go-to person for these parents. Be the person you wish you'd had to guide you when your children were infants or teenagers and gave you sleepless nights at both these stages and those in between.

If you're looking for a way to help people by passing down the knowledge you've accumulated over the years, consider mentoring. It's a great way to share your talents and abilities with someone who sorely needs your help.

90. Volunteer to Assist Older People

"If you want to lift yourself up, lift up someone else."—Booker T. Washington

Are you looking for another way to add meaning to your life? Assisting the elderly in any way you can think of will improve their quality of life and enrich yours. You can find organizations in your neighborhood that welcome volunteers, such as Meals on Wheels, senior centers, and adult day care facilities. Look on the Web, and plug in your state and the words *volunteer to help seniors* to match your interests to a program that appeals to you.

Your state's agency on aging lists several organizations geared specifically to the elderly. Volunteers serving these groups help older people with questions about finances, housing, and insurance. They also advise seniors and their caregivers on any questions they have related to the aging process. You'll find that these organizations deliver a variety of services to older people and their families like giving them the opportunity to use a peer-led telephone program that provides a link for lonely seniors and those who are homebound with the outside world.

If your expertise lies in business, SCORE (Service Corps of Retired Executives) gives free advice to small business owners and prospective business owners about starting a dream business or operating an already established business. In addition to giving in-person advice, they offer online counseling, which would suit you if you enjoy using a computer and working from home.

There's also a great demand in life care communities for volunteers. Many of the residents (especially in the assisted living and nursing divisions) long for social contact and interaction on a regular basis. Short visits and friendly conversation on light-hearted topics often become the highlight of a senior's day. People who live in senior communities would enjoy listening to their favorite music or watching a comedy show with you. Taking part in a favorite pastime with someone else adds an extra dimension of pleasure to the experience; more importantly, older people love having a friend with whom to laugh, share stories, and commiserate.

Many life care communities and senior centers provide activities like handicrafts, book clubs, and lunch/brunch outings to keep the elderly interested and involved while others cater to people with specific disabilities, such as visual impairment. As you can see, many ways to help older people exist in your area. All you have to do is choose one that complements your talents and schedule.

91. Inspire Young People

"It is less painful to learn in youth than to be ignorant in age."—Proverb

You can inspire young people and change their lives in ways that will stay with them for years to come. Many programs pair seniors with young people who range in age from elementary to high school. Retired people work one-on-one with children in schools, helping them with reading, math, and other basics.

In the process, tutors provide students with additional benefits such as improved confidence, self-reliance, and a love of learning. This personal interaction helps the student understand and appreciate the subject in a way that being in a classroom full of students could never provide. Schools in your neighborhood also offer before and after school programs that need extra help.

Other venues also provide opportunities to inspire young people and motivate them to grow academically and socially. Religious organizations offer volunteers the chance to teach faith-based classes on weekends, nights, and during the summer. If you enjoy talking about your faith and explaining it in a way that will appeal to kids, ask your church or synagogue what you can do to help. With younger children these activities often involve arts and crafts projects and using workbooks to teach about religious beliefs. Discussions, group projects, and social activities frequently characterize programs for middle and high school students.

Scouting organizations appreciate having volunteers help students work on badges that stress skill-building and character development. If you don't have much time, making an appearance as a guest speaker on an area of expertise, such as business, sports, or your lifelong career can enlighten and encourage young women to pursue their own dreams.

If you choose to work with young people, you will not only teach them the basic skills they need to help them thrive in their future careers, but you will also inspire them to form positive relationships with you and their peers and to develop the desirable personality traits that you model for them, such as courtesy, kindness, and empathy. Your helpful spirit may encourage them to pay it forward by helping their peers or younger children with subjects they find challenging or by introducing another child to a new skill or hobby in which they excel.

Think about inspiring a child. Nothing keeps you young like working with kids. And they'll make you see the world as you never have before. Best of all, you'll have fun. Any problems you have will lighten as you talk, laugh, and learn with young people.

92. Find Your Own Way to Reach Out to Others

Think of simple things you can do to reach out to people in small ways that make a big difference in their lives. Here are some ways requiring very little time that you can use to help others on a daily basis.

You can start out by telling friends or family members how much you appreciate them. Give specific rather than general thanks such as, "Thanks for what you did," or "Thanks for everything." A general thank-you, like non-specific praise, doesn't tell the person you're thanking what you're grateful for, and the recipient of your gratitude needs to hear exactly what that is.

For example, if a friend gives you a shiny new silver necklace, you can respond by saying something like this: "Your necklace goes with all my clothes, and people tell me it brings out the blue in my eyes. I would have chosen this for myself. Thanks." Maybe your partner takes over a chore you don't enjoy doing, such as the laundry. You could say how much you appreciate the fact that he cares for you enough to perform a chore you dislike.

It also helps to say "You're welcome" after a person thanks you instead of minimizing the expression of gratitude with "No problem," or "It was nothing." It was something. Sometimes our language fails us when we want to express our true feelings; for example when responding to gratitude.

If you want to spread more happiness, pay a friend, family member, or worker, such as a food server, a sincere compliment. Again, avoid general statements such as "I like your shirt," or "Great service!" Instead, say to a friend, "That turquoise top looks striking with your brown skirt," or to the server, "You made eating here a pleasure. You delivered our food quickly, and we appreciated the extra hot rolls."

Say you're in a public place and you see someone having a problem maneuvering a wheel chair or juggling groceries. Ask, "Would you like some help with that?" Then be guided by whether the person accepts or declines your offer. In the same way, if a friend or family member is having a problem, ask what you can do to help, but be specific in your offer.

You can say, "If you want, I'll be over tomorrow to keep your mother company so you can get out for a while. What time do you need me?" or "I know how nervous you are about going for that medical test. I'd be happy to drive you." As always, when you offer help, give the recipient a choice as to whether to accept your offer or to say she doesn't need help at this time.

Another thing you can do is volunteer to read periodically to someone whose eyesight is failing. Look online for organizations for the blind that seek volunteers to provide one-on-one reading sessions to the blind or to record for the blind.

Our mothers used to bake cakes for neighbors as a symbol of love and support during the happy and sad times in their lives. If you want to repeat this kindness but don't have time to bake a cake, buy some fancy cupcakes and brew a fresh pot of coffee or tea for a friend in need. Provide warm support and happy conversation. You'll cheer someone up and feel better yourself.

When some of us were growing up, there used to be a TV show called "Queen for a Day" in which a woman had her every wish granted. Make a special woman in your life "Queen for a Day." The day can be a regular day or a special one like a birthday. Do the recipient of the honor's hair, nails, and make-up, or give her a gift certificate to have it professionally done. Take her to lunch and spend time discussing her favorite topics. Make the day all about her for a regal treatment she'll always remember.

How can you reach out to another person? What can you do to make one person's day (and life) better? Think about how you can help someone today; your action can be planned or spontaneous. You'll find it easy to do and will reap many rewards for the recipient of your kindness and also for yourself.

93. Discover Meaning in Your Existence

"Life may not be the party we'd hoped for, but while we're here we should dance."—Unknown

When you think about what imparts meaning to your life, you'll probably say it's a combination of different components: your family, friends, interests, dreams fulfilled and dreams you're waiting to fulfill. Although you may already embrace all these good things, you long for an even better future. If you have faith in an afterlife, you believe that you'll reunite with those you've loved and lost. If you don't think there's anything after this life, you center your life around the here and now. Whatever you believe, you'll want to think about what makes your life meaningful.

To some women, it may mean not having to worry about money, while to others it may mean giving and receiving love. To most of us, it signifies a combination of these and other things we deem important. Take the time to write in your journal about what gives meaning to your life. Also, think about how in the future you can discover even greater meaning in your life.

Along the way, most of us come to the realization that our relationships impart the deepest meaning to our lives. Ask yourself what you can do to improve the quality of your relationships and how you can minimize the serious conflicts and stresses that sometimes spring from your interactions with those important to you.

Another aspect to finding more meaning in our existence is figuring out how we can contribute to those we love and to society as a whole and how we can leave a lasting impression on the world with our unique talents. Here are some simple things you can do to bring more meaning to your life: play or sing beautiful music to uplift or console someone you care about; create beautiful memories with your grandchildren doing things you both enjoy; write original poems to honor people in your life on special occasions or for no reason at all; or cook specialties that you're known for and share your secret recipes. Find out what you can do to help others in your own distinctive way, and do more of it to create a better life for yourself and those around you.

The meaning we attain in our lives is also closely tied to what brings us the most satisfaction and happiness. Promise yourself today that you'll do more of those things that bring you feelings of delight and accomplishment. Why put them off? Think of three things you've always wanted to do and never got around to that will add meaning to your life. Record them in your journal, and vow to try them. If you put it in writing, you'll be more likely to do so.

Have you thought about trying to locate a childhood friend but put it out of your mind because you didn't know how to begin? Have you wanted to try karaoke but hesitated for fear of making a fool of yourself? Do you long to dance in public but worry about how you'd look? Whatever it is you've wanted to try, this is the right time to try it.

Go ahead. Dare yourself to do something different. It will open up a whole new world to you, and you'll wonder why you didn't start sooner.

Think about the quote that launched this section. Let's face the facts. No one gets everything she wants, but we can all make our best attempt to gain the maximum meaning from our lives, not once in a while, but every single day. While we're here, we need to make our lives as meaningful as possible. While we're here, we should dance.

Chapter 7. Takeaways

- Pinpoint what "the good life" means to you.

- Take the time to examine and re-evaluate your belief systems.

- Research ways of developing your intuition.

- Read self-help books as a positive first step in addressing your problems.

- Turn to blogs and social media that complement your interests to inspire and motivate yourself.

- Tune into non-verbal signals, and listen actively to help build rapport with those you're helping.

- Consider mentoring someone. Help others by passing down knowledge you've accumulated over the years.

- Contact your state's council on aging to find opportunities to help the elderly.

- Work with young people to help them develop positive personality traits in addition to academic skills.

- Be specific rather than general when you thank or compliment someone.

Chapter 8: Put It All Together

94. Use a Systematic Approach to Realize Your Dreams

"It is never too late to be what you might have been."—*George Eliot (AKA Mary Anne Evans)*

By this time, you're probably thinking about how you can make everything click and come together so that you can start living your best life now. To get you where you want to go, think about building a systematic plan that helps you mobilize all your resources to assist you in reaching each goal you want to accomplish.

In other words, develop a strategy that will take you from Point A to Point B. One way to do this easily is to draw up a plan in which you write exactly what you'll need to do to reach your goals. Head your paper with the words *Goal, Dream Job (Hobby or Activity)*. Next, describe your proposed goal, dream job, hobby, or activity. Create a strategy for as many goals as you have. Once you've recorded your goals and how you plan to accomplish them, draw up a list of potential obstacles that you think may pose a problem to you in reaching your goals. Call this section *Potential Obstacles and Rebuttals*, and place it after the strategies section. This list reflects your scaredy cat self, not your real self that continues to grow in self-confidence every day.

Leave three or four lines after each scaredy cat statement you make. In this space you'll write a rebuttal to each statement you made in your Potential Obstacles list. This will consist of a reason why you won't let each negative thought deter you from getting to your goal.

Here's an example of how you'll draw up your systematic approach to realizing a goal you set for yourself, along with rebuttals to potential obstacles:

Goal: To Start My Own Jewelry Business

Dream Job: Making necklaces and earrings to sell at home shows, craft fairs, and online stores

Strategy: What I Need to Do

1. Talk to a friend who's in the business about marketing my products, and consult an organization that advises seniors about starting a business.

2. Seek advice about marketing from reputable online sources.

3. Look for craft shows where I can display my products. Survey friends and acquaintances about their interest in attending a jewelry show in my home or at a fair. Which do most of them prefer?

4. Make sample products to display at home shows and craft fairs.

5. Look into online sales outlets to see what I have to do about marketing and selling my jewelry.

6. Figure out whether I have the advertising know-how to depict and sell my products online. If not, who can help me and what will it cost?

Potential Obstacles and Rebuttals

1. My jewelry may not appeal to a wide range of buyers. **Rebuttal**: I need to do research in advance to study current trends to see if my product is in keeping with them, yet unique enough to appeal to different people.

2. I've never sold anything in my life. How do I know if I have the personality for it? **Rebuttal**: I have the desire to sell my jewelry and act enthusiastic about my pieces. That should count for something. Also, many strangers compliment me when I wear pieces I've made.

3. I don't know how to market my products on online sales outlets. **Rebuttal:** I can ask someone who sells online or by researching it.

You can see by this example that it helps to draw up a strategy and a plan to implement it before you begin to make your dream job or hobby a reality. Write out a self-talk script similar to the one that you see in the Obstacle/Rebuttal section, and use it to banish any impediments you think will block your plan. Then start moving on your plan, and do your best to make it happen.

95. Overcome Temporary Setbacks

"Never give up. Keep your thoughts and your mind always on the goal. One of the secrets of success is to refuse to let temporary setbacks defeat you."—Unknown

Everything we've discussed in this book requires strength and courage, qualities you've needed and demonstrated over the years to transport you through the many challenges that confronted you, such as leaving a job and starting a new one, adjusting to your children leaving home or returning home, or grieving the loss of someone dear to you. As we grow older, we sometimes begin to question our resilience in springing back from life events like these and wonder if we're capable of overcoming the emotional fallout from the problems we come up against along the way.

We also think about our ability to confront setbacks when trying to reach certain goals that we've been striving to accomplish, such as trying to re-enter a job market composed mainly of young people. Also, in our personal lives we may have suffered some major disappointments that have made us more vulnerable. A relative, friend, or business associate may have hurt or betrayed us in some way, so we find ourselves becoming more cautious in dealing with people.

No matter what experience you've had that may have cut into your courage and confidence in attaining your dream, you can renew these qualities in yourself by practicing goal setting and motivating self-talk. Be willing to take the steps necessary to help your goals materialize. If you harbor a strong intention and persevere, you can realize all the goals we've discussed in this book: improving your health, expanding your mind, nurturing your relationships, seeking and discovering more joy in your life, and facing your challenges gracefully.

When temporary setbacks cut into your plans, make a forceful effort to meet them head on; don't let them stand in the way of arriving at the place you want to be. Imagine you're starting a new business and you haven't had much luck with your online sales.

Consider hiring someone with marketing skills to list your information on the site, and see how that works. If it doesn't, try sales outlets that handle merchandise similar to yours, like small shops or kiosks at the mall. Persist until you get to where you want to be.

Losing or gaining weight can also present temporary setbacks. The main problem facing most women regarding weight loss or gain comes when they don't see results as quickly as they'd like. Patience and tenacity will tide you over if you allow these virtues to guide you as you have in the past when stumbling blocks surfaced. Make haste at a slow pace; don't rush things. But don't give up. If "Plan A" doesn't work, give "Plan B" a fair chance. Never stop trying to reach your goal.

After retirement, some women constantly grapple with feelings of depression or sadness and can't lift themselves up no matter how strong their efforts. Reassure yourself that your frustration is a temporary setback and know that you will find a way to enjoy an emotionally balanced life. You can find a way to conquer any emotional problems that cross your path. Showing the same sticktoitiveness you displayed many times in your life in the past will help you find an answer.

You can overcome whatever impediments try to block you from reaching your goals. You have the strength and staying power to find a way to remove whatever is standing in your way. Make up your mind to overcome temporary setbacks now.

96. Modify Your Goals if Necessary

"When my kids left home, I had more time on my hands, so I decided to start my own catering business. After a while, I could see that my business wasn't growing as I'd hoped because of a lot of competition in the area. I made the decision to scale it down and limit it to baking cakes for special occasions. In a short time, things picked up, and I hired a helper. Sometimes you have to change your original plan to make it work out the way you want."—Loretta, age 60, fancy cake baker, Naples, Florida

You've tried "Plan A" and moved on to "Plan B," but your new idea for a part-time business didn't work out as you'd hoped. You can choose to give it up entirely, or you can modify your goals and expectations and go on to another plan. In your journal, brainstorm a variety of ways you can modify your goals without compromising your original idea. If you're offering a product, you may want to try concentrating on one sales outlet rather than spreading yourself too thin. You also may want to advertise your wares on social media sites and ask people to "like" what you've posted and to share it.

Maybe you're working diligently to learn a foreign language in anticipation of a long-awaited trip to Europe. You're not satisfied with your program that involves using CDs you borrowed from a friend. As an alternative, find an online program that pairs you with a native speaker, or ask your local community college to recommend an English as a Second Language student who would like to exchange practice sessions in your respective languages.

Another situation that may call for modifying your goals could relate to a volunteer organization or board to which you donate your time. If you find you don't like the direction in which the organization is heading, look for another group that better complements your values and core beliefs. Don't think you're a quitter if you leave an organization, even one to which you've been committed for a long time. Be true to yourself, and don't compromise your beliefs for a group whose mission you no longer espouse. Know when it's time to move on.

Suppose one of your goals is to eat more healthy foods. You've tried to exchange your usual favorites, such as burgers and fries, for alternatives like yogurt and healthy cereal. But you're getting bored with the curdled consistency of yogurt, and the flax seed in the cereal is jumpstarting your colon. Try to find different foods that taste more palatable to you, such as whole wheat pasta or a healthy cereal that doesn't cause such potent side effects. Also, allow yourself to eat the foods you hanker for in moderation.

Modifying your goals isn't easy, especially if you've banked on something for a long time or you've worked for an organization for many years and have formed lasting ties with the people there. If you take that leap, you'll often come out better than if you didn't. Sometimes making a change can lead you in new directions that will bring you more satisfaction and less aggravation than you would have gotten if you' had remained static and not moved on to better things.

97. Don't Let the Naysayers Get You Down

"The greatest revenge is to accomplish what others say you cannot do."—Unknown

Whenever you try to do something, there's someone who's going to say it won't work out. Don't let negative people put a damper on anything you want to do, no matter how big or small. How can you manage dealing with naysayers? One thing you can do is vow that you're not going to let them get to you, and let them know that in no uncertain terms, being as tactful as you can, of course.

Below is an example of how Jess, a retired woman dealt with Dawn, a neighbor, who makes a practice of giving all the reasons why someone shouldn't try something different or daring. Jess always wanted to earn her degree in psychology, but put her education on hold when she decided to stay home to raise her kids. Once they were all in school, she found a job as a personnel manager. Recently, she signed up for the spring semester at a local city university that gave her credit for some of her past courses and for life experience.

Jess: If I'm hearing you right, I think you're saying I'm too old to finish my degree because I can't handle the stress of competing with young kids.

Dawn: I didn't say you're old, just too old to start school again at this stage of your life. Let's be realistic. These kids today are way ahead of us, especially when it comes to technology.

Jess: I'm sorry you feel that way. But in a way, I'm glad. You've motivated me to prove you wrong. I'm going to get my degree and maybe even go for a master's when I'm finished with that.

Dawn: I still think you're taking on too much at your age. This is our time to relax, not drive ourselves to an early grave from stress. I don't want to discourage you but...

Jess (cutting her off): It seems like that's exactly what you're doing. I'd appreciate it if you'd support me instead. That's what friends do—right?

Dawn (smiling hesitantly): Well, when you put it that way, I don't feel like I have much of a choice.

Here's another instance of a naysayer trying to discourage a friend. Maria and her husband Matt are planning a romantic getaway to the shore for the weekend. Jade, a friend since high school, is getting tired of hearing Maria talk about how she and her mate are still in love and work to keep their love life alive after forty years together.

Jade: You two never give up, do you? As you've probably guessed, those days are over for Jack and me. We're good companions and that's the way we both like it. We have a history together with the kids and grandkids, and we truly love each other, but not that way. The simple fact is that we don't have the time or energy that we used to for a love life.

Maria: Just because you think you're too old doesn't mean that Matt and I are ready to live like two decrepit people waiting to die.

Jade: Maybe not, but I think there comes a time when you need to adjust to getting older and make a change in your relationship. When your body ages you don't need mad, passionate love to keep your marriage going. You can always cuddle and hold hands. If you ask me, there comes a time when things change, and you need to accept that.

Maria: Maybe that's okay for you, but Matt and I want to keep our love life sizzling for as long as we can. What's wrong with that?

Jade (rolling her eyes): Sorry I mentioned it. Just giving my opinion.

Maria: No, I'm glad you did. It makes me think of how lucky we are to still enjoy going on that romantic weekend together. Maybe you and Jack should consider going on one.

Jade: He'd probably laugh hysterically if I suggested it.

Maria: It's worth a try! You never know. It may open up a whole new world to both of you.

Often, as in the stories above, there's a subtext to naysayers' strong opinions about what you want in your life. It's not hard to see that jealousy or sour grapes is often a prime motivator. When dealing with naysayers, it helps to take what they say lightly and to tell them unequivocally that your opinion is the only one that counts when it comes to living your life exactly the way you want to live it.

98. Take Control of Your Life

"At this stage of the game, I've promised myself I'm taking control of my life. I do only what I want, when I want to. Sure, I still help people the best I can and have a social life, but now I do everything on my own terms. Of course, I can't control my life totally, but I take charge of the things I can. If I can't handle something on my own, I ask for help. I'm not afraid to say no and feel no regrets the way I used to when I wasn't in control. "—Carmella, 70-year-old retired restaurant owner

One of the most appealing aspects of retirement is the knowledge that you'll have more control of your life than you've had in the past. Sometimes, however, we find the things we truly yearn for eluding us.

A dear sister with health problems needs rides to doctor's appointments and treatments on a weekly basis, along with constant moral support; your college roommate wants to visit for a few days and you've planned to tackle a writing project; you and your partner belong to a bowling league that meets weekly, but the two of you would like to schedule more time to do the things you want, like go to the theater; and you also have a long-standing monthly dinner engagement with a couple from your old neighborhood. This has become a sacred ritual by now, but time for your own interests diminishes considerably with this and all the other activities that fill your days.

When will you find time to do all the things you've put on hold? Consider drawing up a plan that allows time for what you want to do, yet gives you the chance to help others and enjoy your social life. The first thing to think about is how many of your commitments are non-negotiable. To which ones do you feel a sense of moral obligation?

For example, if no one else can share the job of transporting your sister, you will, of course, be the one to help her. If there's a possibility that another family member could assist with this task, but hasn't yet come forward to volunteer, ask that person for help. If help isn't forthcoming and you can't handle things alone, you'll need to help yourself by seeking senior services in your area that will advise you on how to get assistance so that you are not totally responsible all of the time.

How will you resolve the issue of a college roommate who wants to visit, especially when you've already planned to tackle a major project? Of course, you want to see her. After all, you were best friends in college, and she's one of your children's godparents. But the time isn't right, given your prior commitment to a task you must complete. If you simply mention that another time would be better, she'll probably understand. While you're talking, you can set a different time for a visit to validate how important her friendship is to you.

The bowling league that your husband and you belong to gives you a chance to enjoy the company of friends, but it takes up a huge chunk of time every week, and that bowling ball is getting mighty heavy. More and more, you find yourself wanting to use that time to do something as a couple, like go to more shows or concerts, but you don't want to hurt the other members' feelings since you've met at that same bowling alley on Friday night for years.

If you feel strongly that you'd like to quit the league, look for a good time to tell your teammates. You can say that you find yourselves so busy lately that couple time has gone by the wayside and that you need a little more togetherness time. You can still see them socially when it's convenient for them and you, but not for bowling. They may laugh and ask if you're serious (hopefully, you are), but your response will have the added benefit of diffusing a potentially awkward situation because of the way you presented it and the way they received it.

How will you handle the monthly dinner date with friends?

Even though it's only once a month, it still eats into the time you and your partner need to pursue your own interests. You could suggest meeting a little less often, say once every two months, and tell them that although you enjoy their company greatly you've been pressed for time lately. Listen to what they say, and if they're not happy with that, see if you can come to an agreement that satisfies all concerned.

You want to help those you love, have an active social life, and, at the same time, to pursue your own interests as an individual and with your partner, but sometimes your commitments to others dominate your days to the extent that the things you love to do fade into the background.

Try to strike is happy medium. You can start by looking at everything you're currently doing. Think of the things you must do (like help relatives) and the things you can scale down (like activities that involve friends and organizations). Consider all the activities you want to do alone and those you want to share with your partner, and then devise a plan that will help you live a full life that encompasses all of the elements you value but at a pace you can live with. Take control of your life. Make what you want to do a priority even if it means saying *no* sometimes, even if it means not always pleasing everyone.

99. Banish Negativity from Your Life

"Isn't it nice to think that tomorrow is a new day with no mistakes in it yet?"—L.M. Montgomery

"I can't." "I don't know how." "I'm afraid." How many times have you let negativity stand in the way of attaining your most cherished dreams? If negative vibes drag you down, start by turning these unhelpful thoughts into positive ones. Every time you impede your own progress in reaching a goal by thinking the worst scenario your pessimistic side can conjure up, banish the thought by using this simple technique. Address the thought assertively with a strong command like "Leave" or "Get out of my way." You can make your command dramatic by saying, "Begone!" or you can give it a silly ring by saying, "Vamoose" or "Skedaddle." You may find that using a dramatic or a light-hearted word makes your negative thought sound not as imposing. It also tends to trivialize it, which is one way of not letting it dominate your life.

You can reinforce your command with a gesture (when you're not in the company of others, of course). You can invent your own gesture or try something like putting your two palms in front of you with a *stop* motion or mimic a karate chop movement with your hand. Alternatively, you can reframe your negative statement into a positive one by saying something to yourself such as, "I can do this" or "I'll find a way."

You may find yourself giving negative messages about your capabilities to others in this vein; "I can't handle everything that's going on in my life now." "I don't know how to help my child."; or, "I'm afraid I'll get the cancer that killed my mother." Whether you proclaim these damaging statements to yourself or to others, it's time to think about how they can easily become self-fulfilling prophecies. If you replay these scripts enough times, they will infiltrate your life, presenting impassable roadblocks to your happiness and sense of well-being.

When you're tempted to voice these pessimistic thoughts to others, change them into positive statements. For example, referencing the previously mentioned examples of negative statements, you can change these thoughts into more constructive statements. "I'm experiencing some heavy problems now, but I have faith I'll come through everything." "My daughter is going through a bitter divorce. Sometimes I'm not sure of how to help her, but I'll do whatever I can and hope for the best." And, "Naturally, I think about getting cancer because my mother had it, but I'll keep up with my check-ups and preventive care. That helps reassure me."

We can't totally obliterate negative thoughts, but when they dog us, we can do our best to spin them into more hopeful thoughts that will set us on our way to living the life we want and deserve. Program your mind with sunny, upbeat thoughts that will move you forward to everything you want to experience in your life.

100. Make Each Day a New Adventure

"Do one thing every day that scares you."—Eleanor Roosevelt

Do you wake up each day to a sense of anticipation of what's to come? If not, making a few simple changes will take you where you want to go. Try starting your day with a familiar prayer or one you write yourself. Give thanks for what you have. If you'd prefer, meditate for a few minutes.

Follow the plan you've created for your day (See section #13 of Chapter Two). But every so often, scrap your plan and wing it. Live serendipitously: ask your partner to accompany you to a place you've always longed to see, or call a friend on the spur of the moment and ask if she'd like to see a movie or take a long, scenic walk through the park. If she's busy and you have no one else to ask, go by yourself.

Even though waking up and going to sleep at the same time every day promotes good health, varying your routine occasionally makes life less predictable and more of an adventure. Try changing your patterns in small ways to refresh and energize yourself. If you usually work on a favorite project in the morning, switch to the afternoon or evening. Experiment to see how it affects your productivity and sense of satisfaction in performing your task.

Did you ever want to make a change from being a morning person to a night person or vice versa? Why not try it? Even though you've always thought of yourself as a lark or an owl, you may surprise yourself and feel comfortable trying a new approach. If you find you don't enjoy waking up early or staying up late, you can go back to the way you've always done things.

Try eating breakfast for dinner or forget about making lunch (you didn't feel like it anyway), and go to a restaurant you love instead. Eat dinner for lunch or lunch for dinner for a week. If you like the change, make it permanent.

Write in your journal about things you can do to add a sense of adventure. What can you do that will liven up your life to the extent that you'll notice a difference in how you spend your days? What would it take to make today and every day a new adventure?

101. Live Your Dream Now

"Start by doing what is necessary; then do what's possible; and suddenly you're doing the impossible."—St. Francis of Assisi

Do you want to start living your dream today? There's nothing stopping you but the fears and limitations you place on yourself. Fears are nothing but illusions and cannot prevent you from doing what you want if you don't give them power over you. The truth is if you allow yourself to take the necessary steps, you can begin to live the life you long for, starting this very moment. You can make your retirement years the best time of your life, filled with the warmth of loving relationships, steadfast friendships, and stimulating activities.

Here are some specific steps you can take to start living your best life now. Identify what's important to you. If you're doing things now that you wouldn't miss substantially if you didn't have them, think about eliminating them or engaging in them less frequently. Spend the bulk of your time on the people, activities, and projects you value most.

Reevaluate your priorities on a regular basis, and change them accordingly. Let's say you enjoyed spending time on a certain hobby but, as time goes by, you don't find it as interesting. Think about moving on to something that engages you more strongly. It's important to give whatever activity you try a fair chance, but if you decide it doesn't hold your interest, it doesn't mean you've failed, but rather that you've made a change to something you liked better. Change takes courage that you already possess if you're willing to tap into it.

Here's something else you can do to start living your dream. Accomplish routine and mundane tasks as quickly and efficiently as possible. Do you detest paying bills or doing housework? Make up your mind to get the jobs you dread most out of the way so that you can enjoy your free time.

We tend to procrastinate when it comes to doing tasks we don't like. If you decide to dig in and perform tasks without delay, you'll find a new sense of freedom because the jobs you dislike won't drag you down since you'll get them done quickly. The more time you spend thinking about arduous chores rather than actually getting started on them, the more time you'll waste. Tackle those jobs you find distasteful, and you'll be one step closer to spending time doing things you enjoy.

Another thing you can do to bring you closer to your dream is to avoid wasting time worrying and complaining. Most of the worries we harbor are grounded in fears and don't mean anything. Their only purpose is making us lose valuable time and energy in reaching our goals. Did you ever notice how worry saps energy, ambition, and the ability to relax and enjoy your life?

If you have a legitimate worry, consider all aspects of the situation, talk to someone you trust, and search for an answer. Whatever you do, don't let worry dominate your life. Worrying doesn't help solve your problem and only makes you feel helpless and hopeless, the opposite of what you're seeking if you're aiming to de-stress, reinvent, and fire up your life.

Likewise, complaining makes us appear disagreeable and bad-tempered. Consider how we feel about ourselves when we complain. Often slight aches and pains escalate to unbearable levels. Minor illnesses reach catastrophic levels in our imagination when we let our complaints get out of control. We can also easily blow out of proportion things another person did to hurt or offend us, making that person one we should shun and avoid at all costs. Complaining brings us down, and doesn't help us move our plan forward for the best life possible.

Are you ready to live your dream now? If you read every section of this book, add your own personal touches and apply them to your own life, you will find retirement years the best years of your life. That's a promise. You have everything you need and you can do everything it takes to live your best life now. I wish you *bon voyage* along the way.

Chapter 8: Takeaways

- Draw up a strategy and plan and implement it to realize your dreams.

- Face temporary setbacks head-on. Don't let them stand in your way.

- Modify your goals and move on to others if what you want to do isn't working out to your satisfaction.

- Take lightly what naysayers tell you. Tell them that your opinion is the one that counts when it comes to living your life.

- Take control of your life, and make what you want to do a priority, even if it means not pleasing everyone.

- Turn negative thoughts into helpful ones to set you on your way to living the life you want and deserve.

- Try changing your daily patterns in small ways to refresh and energize yourself.

- Spend the bulk of your time on the people, activities, and projects you value most.

Quiz # 6: Live a Meaningful Life and Put It All Together

Here's a quiz on the final two chapters. After the quiz, you'll find a final evaluation that you can answer in your journal so that you can review what you wrote periodically. Take the time to write your answers in prose, poetry, or art, whichever suits you best. It will give you an idea of where you are in the process of re-inventing your life.

And now, on to the quiz. How do you feel about living a meaningful life? To what degree is it your most important goal? Have you put together everything we've talked about in this book and decided upon a systematic approach that will help you live your best life possible in your retirement? Moreover, have you added your unique experiences and original ideas to help you discover what it means for you personally to live a meaningful life?

1. For many of us "the good life" means

   a) lying on a sunny beach with a Margarita in one hand and a steamy novel in the other.
   b) finding whatever brings you the most excitement, thrills, and chills.
   c) finding the most happiness by loving and being loved by family and friends.

2. Examining our broader belief systems will lead us to

   a) a decision to completely change our views about religion, politics, and social issues.
   b) question everything we ever held true.
   c) an assessment of our beliefs about politics, religion, and social issues.

3. An authoritative self-help book written by an expert can

   a) provide you with more help than going to therapy or talking with a friend.
   b) help reassure you when you're feeling nervous about your problems.
   c) present a positive first step in discussing practical solutions to improve your life.

4. To find inspirational books relevant to your interests,

   a) browse in a bookstore and choose the book with the most interesting book jacket.

   b) go to the library and choose a book on your topic by finding the person with the best credentials. Look at their personal experience.

   c) look in a search engine and type in *inspirational books* and the topic that interests you most.

5. Tuning into non-verbal signals when someone is telling you a problem helps you

   a) know exactly what kind of advice to give.

   b) get to know the person you're assisting.

   c) build a stronger rapport with the person you're helping.

6. Mentoring someone is a great way to

   a) build up your confidence by showing the person you're helping how much you know.

   b) prove to people that you're doing something constructive in your retirement.

   c) share your talents and abilities with someone who needs your help.

7. When an older person takes part in a favorite pastime with a volunteer,

   a) it makes the older person feel a sense of sadness when the volunteer leaves.

   b) it gives the older person a break from Bingo and canasta.

   c) it adds an extra dimension of pleasure to the experience and gives the older person a friend with whom to share stories and laughter.

8. If you work with young people, you'll help them

   a) listen to the teacher and stop causing problems in school.
   b) stay out of trouble because they'd feel guilty if they let you down.
   c) develop positive relationships and personality traits you model for them.

9. If someone has a problem, ask what you can do to help, and

   a) do only the jobs you like best—forget about cooking and cleaning.
   b) wait for the person to call you and say she's ready. Maybe she won't remember.
   c) be specific in your offer about what you'll do to assist the person.

10. What usually imparts the deepest meaning to our lives?

    a) Making a lot of money doing what we love best
    b) Our most significant and dearest memories
    c) Our relationships

11. Start living your best life now by

    a) doing whatever you feel like doing each day. Why over-plan in such an uncertain world?
    b) putting away as much money as you can for the future and not touching it.
    c) drawing up a systematic plan, creating a strategy, and implementing it.

12. Renew your courage and confidence in the face of setbacks by practicing

    a) practicality. Maybe what you want is a fantasy.

b) patience. Don't act too quickly as things may get worse.

c) goal-setting and motivating self-talk.

13. Sometimes modifying your goals can

a) make you feel like you gave up too soon. It's best to stay with your original idea.

b) discourage you from staying with your original plan.

c) lead you in a new direction that will bring you more satisfaction.

14. When dealing with naysayers

a) listen to what they say. They may have a point.

b) ignore them and maybe they'll go away.

c) take what they say lightly, and tell them your opinion is the one that counts.

15. When taking control of your life,

a) be sure to fill up your social calendar to overflowing. Have fun—you're retired.

a) always put others first and yourself second. Being selfish is unbecoming.

c) make what you want to do a priority.

16. When a negative thought about what you're trying to do invades your mind,

a) curse a blue streak at it, and don't worry about who hears you.

b) put it out of your mind immediately.

c) address the thought with a strong command and a gesture to match.

17. Varying your routine occasionally makes life

a) more stressful and unbearable.
b) a new experience which you may or may not enjoy. It's a toss-up.
c) less predicable and more adventurous.

18. The main issues stopping you from living your dreams are

a) comments your friends make when they hear what you want to accomplish.
b) obstacles like money, time, and energy that stand in your way.
c) the fears and limitations you place on yourself.

Answers

Mostly A's: Think more carefully about what you need to do to live a more meaningful life. Listen to yourself before you listen to anyone else. Don't think about giving up so easily on your dreams. Set your goals and stay with them if they're working out. If they're not, find it in yourself to change your course of action and revise your original plan. Live adventurously, and don't be afraid to vary your routine. Nothing and no one but yourself can hold you back. You have all the qualities you need right now to live a meaningful life, your best life. All you have to do is make your good qualities; namely, strength, perseverance, and optimism, start working for you. Promise yourself you'll begin now without delay.

Mostly B's: Consider thinking more deeply about how to live your best life now. Bring yourself up to the next level, and ask yourself exactly how you can start moving forward on an individualized plan that will help you fire up your life in retirement.

Work at becoming a more intuitive listener to the people you're assisting. Be willing to reevaluate and modify your goals if things aren't going as planned. Practice acting more assertively with naysayers. You can easily do all these things by putting forth a stronger effort. That effort will make all the difference in achieving the most meaningful life you can live during your retirement years.

Mostly C's: You're on the best path possible to living a meaningful life in retirement. You consult authoritative sources when you need information about reaching your goals. You know how to attain a sense of purpose by helping and mentoring others. You also deal with the negativity of setbacks and naysayers effectively and always come out on top. Best of all, you know what you want and how to get it by applying a systematic, organized plan of action.

Final Evaluation

As a final exercise, write in your journal about what you hope to do during your retirement that you never had the time or nerve to try before. What do you not want in your life any longer? State it in no uncertain terms. If you'd prefer, write a free-flowing poem describing what you want and how to achieve it. Another alternative is to draw pictures or to create a timeline or diagram of what you hope to accomplish.

Keep your writing, timeline, or art in a special place, and look back on it every month or so to see if you're on the right path. If not, figure out what you need to do to get there. I have every confidence you will meet all of your goals and lead a happy, exciting, and fulfilling life from this day forward. Godspeed.